HOW TO HOLD
YOUR JOB

PRENTICE-HALL INTERNATIONAL, INC., *London*
PRENTICE-HALL OF AUSTRALIA PTY. LIMITED, *Sydney*
PRENTICE-HALL CANADA INC., *Toronto*
PRENTICE-HALL OF INDIA PRIVATE LIMITED, *New Delhi*
PRENTICE-HALL OF JAPAN, INC., *Tokyo*
PRENTICE-HALL OF SOUTHEAST ASIA PTE. LTD., *Singapore*
WHITEHALL BOOKS LIMITED, *Wellington, New Zealand*
EDITORA PRENTICE-HALL DO BRASIL LTDA., *Rio de Janeiro*

Arnold R. Deutsch

HOW TO HOLD YOUR JOB

GAINING SKILLS AND BECOMING PROMOTABLE IN DIFFICULT TIMES

Prentice-Hall, Inc., Englewood Cliffs, New Jersey 07632

Library of Congress Cataloging in Publication Data

Deutsch, Arnold (date)
    How to hold your job.

    "A Spectrum Book."
    Bibliography: p.
    Includes index.
    1. Vocational guidance.   2. Job security.   3. Pro-
motions.   I. Title.
HF5381.D4542   1984   650.1' 4   83-21228
ISBN 0-13-410621-0
ISBN 0-13-410613-X (pbk.)

*I much appreciate the editorial assistance
provided by Dr. Susan Shwartz
in the preparation of the manuscript for this book.*

1 2 3 4 5 6 7 8 9 10

ISBN 0-13-410621-0

ISBN 0-13-410613-X {PBK.}

Editorial/production supervision by William P. O'Hearn
Cover design by Hal Siegel
Manufacturing buyer: Edward J. Ellis

Contents

HOW TO HOLD YOUR JOB

Introduction

Getting a job—or keeping it—shouldn't be the hardest job you'll ever have to face. There are times, however, when that seems to be the case. The past few years have unfortunately been one of those times. As numerous headlines in 1982 and 1983 have told us, unemployment has been at its highest point since the end of World War II. But you don't need headlines to tell you that. Whether you're working now, are looking for work, or are a student anticipating (with some reasonable fear) the day you'll enter the world of work, you know that the job market has been tough.

Despite the anticipated upturn, the tight market has fostered a desperation mentality among workers at all levels. Students frequently don't take any courses for which they don't see an immediate dollars-and-cents payoff. Economic and employment conditions have forced many people to revise their expectations and, in some cases, to abandon cherished ambitions for more "realistic" goals.

On the job the desperation mentality is expressed in many ways: Don't rock the boat; hang on as long as you can; play it safe; don't ask for the moon. Depressing, isn't it? It needn't be—not in the long run. Before you resign yourself to simply scraping by, think again. It's possible that your present job, even if you don't like it now, can be transformed from "just a paycheck and a dental plan" into a valuable stage in your career growth. How can you go about this?

Today people are examining the world of work and writing down what they find. Work itself has become a subject to study, to learn about. More than ever before, books on job-related subjects are available—the one you're reading now, for example. Why? Because in our economy, which is fast shifting from production-oriented to information-based, there is a crying need for more and better information on a topic people consider vitally important: how to hold a job, how to enrich it, and how to move up the promotion ladder.

Anyone who's ever held a paying job knows, for example, that doing the tasks for which he or she was hired is only a small part of the job. Workers who are valuable employees are good at two things: technical competence and "people skills." People skills involve communication, negotiation, and simply getting along with coworkers and superiors. If you feel that you need a refresher course in people skills (or as MBA jargon calls them, "organizational behavior"), Part I, "Holding a Job," is the place to turn to. Here you'll find guides on how to upgrade productivity through faster reading, better concentration, and more accurate remembering. You'll find practical advice on how to behave in the high-pressure business community, including how to be assertive, but not "pushy"; and how to survive at work despite a problem boss, manipulative colleagues, or even an inconsiderate office mate who puffs smoke in your face.

Preparing for the World of Work

"What do you *want* to do?" A century ago, no one really bothered to ask. Preparing for a job was simple. As soon as you got old enough and strong enough to handle the same tasks (generally hard labor) that your mother and father performed, you pitched in. If work wasn't exciting and didn't make you think, at least you knew—barring war, pestilence, and famine—what you were going to do when you became an adult. Did you like the job you "inherited"? Never mind that! A job was a job. Even today many people think of work as if they were born in 1800. These people, although they call themselves "realists," simply are not being realistic. Today potential workers face a dizzying array of options, of training, and of career paths. And the way we look at work has changed just as dramatically. Workers don't think of jobs as mechanical sets of tasks performed by interchangeable, expendable workers; smart workers think of careers that will provide not only a living wage but self-respect and personal satisfaction. And more often than not, their management agrees with them.

Part II of this book, "Moving Ahead," offers you strategies designed to help you thrive in today's challenging work environment. Do you want to make a career shift into one of the high tech industries? How do you go about getting the right training? What about moving to the Sunbelt, just as you've always dreamed of? Then there are on-the-job issues such as choosing a mentor, "working smarter," refining communication skills, and—not least of all—knowing when, why, and how to move on . . . and up.

New Directions

Perhaps you're familiar with the old Chinese curse, "May you live in interesting times." Part III, "Options and Directions," ought to make you see that living in interesting times is a blessing, not a curse. This section challenges many of the assumptions we all make about work. After all, why can't you shift careers at forty? If you're female, why do you have to work a pink-collar job (unless you want to) when blue-collar jobs pay better? And assuming you're healthy enough to take it, why shouldn't you moonlight to bring in extra cash?

As this part will show you, these are challenging times during which workers and managers alike are reexamining work and all the truisms about it.

Living and Working in the Real World

Although American men and women spend the greater portion of their adult lives working, they usually enter the work force unprepared by either parents or schools to face the everyday realities of a job. They place great emphasis on the kind of work they do, but most of them start out without having the faintest idea of how to make satisfying career choices. They're bombarded with information, yet are not taught how to look for a job systematically. They're indoctrinated with the value of getting ahead, but are largely unaware of how to get what they want from their workplaces, their pay envelopes, their colleagues, and their bosses.

If you're saying to yourself at this point, "I don't want to put up with being uninformed any more," this book is for you. But before you read any further, before you even so much as glance at any of the sections (or at the bibliography of books on everything from job hunting to government agencies), take time out and ask yourself three questions.

- How stable is my present job?
- Do I like what I do?
- Do I know what I'm going to do next?

If you've answered "No" or "I don't know" to any one of those questions, this book is for you. The first thing you'll learn from it is that your job is something that you *do*, not something that does a job *on* you.

How do you change from victim to victor in the work area? No one book can possibly give you an answer to that question; this one won't even try. What it will give you is information on how to make rational and informed choices about your work life.

So good reading—and good luck!

HOLDING A JOB

Consider the following cases. You worked hard in school, got good marks, and were rewarded with interviews, job offers, and, finally, this great new position. Or you were a success at your last job, so this new one—with its pay increase, higher level of responsibilities, greater visibility, *and* demand for your special skills—looks like a sure thing. So, in either case, can we conclude that if you're good at what you do, all you have to do is go right in and do it?

No!

Sure, competence—even excellence—at what you do is vital. Otherwise you and your résumé can't hope to survive a preliminary screening. And you know about people skills: after all, didn't you charm the interviewers? So you got the job. But now, unless you're a hermit or in some field that requires no contact with coworkers, you're likely to find that the mechanics of getting a job done, such as talking to people, coping with their problems and yours, and running into conflicting needs, are as important as the work itself.

"Working smarter" is a theme in this book. In this section, "working smarter" has two meanings. First, it means upgrading on-the-job skills, such as concentration, listening, remembering, and reading. Second, "working smarter" means dealing more effectively with coworkers: overcoming your own shyness or a difficult boss; or standing up for yourself if someone harasses you sexually, tries to back you into a political blind alley, or even makes you sick because he (or she) smokes, and you're allergic to tobacco.

At this point, old-fashioned people and even well-meaning friends will tell you, "Don't be so sensitive." But unresolved difficulties with coworkers can lower your morale, increase stress and on-the-job fatigue, and sink your level of productivity. As for those "little, picky details" you frequently underestimate, remember that they're part of your work, too. People and picky details: they're all part of your job, and you should try to deal with them as competently as you do the rest of it.

1

Improving Your on-the-Job Performance

Bringing Creativity to Your Job

Have you ever felt pulled apart inside by the force of rules, regulations, and patterns in the workplace? If so, the problem could be that you're a creative individual with a natural inclination to move at your own pace, to do things in new and different ways.

As an idea person, you might have come up with a terrific, as well as a *workable*, idea for streamlining some activity in your department. When the time came to present your idea, you might have been charged with enthusiasm and eager to see it tried, even on an experimental basis. Unless you presented your idea to another creative individual, its chances of getting off the ground were poor; your chances of feeling blocked and frustrated were extremely high.

If you are that peculiar being, the creative person, you probably know it. You've always existed in a realm where ideas flow freely. Scientists have found the typical creative person to be intelligent, independent, open to new ideas and experiences, intrigued by complexity, shunning routine, intuitive, and motivated.

If that sounds like you, perhaps you've experienced some of the frustrations described above. You'd probably *like* to bring more of your natural creativity to your job. Given creative career outlets, you could perform all your tasks more efficiently. Your employer would benefit, too. Unfortunately, no guidelines have been developed for creative people who experience frustration in their jobs.

Until now!

The ideal situation, of course, is to find an employer determined to foster creativity. Some exist, but it may take a while to find them. Another option is to break away from your traditional job and become self-employed in some creative occupation, which could lead to starvation. While exploring these and other alternatives, you may find the following suggestions helpful:

1. *Don't be afraid of being labeled strange.* Creative people sometimes feel rejected. Discovering new forms, symbols, and patterns requires a special kind of courage.

2. *Manage your time and workspace creatively.* Some jobs allow the individual great flexibility, others very little; but some freedom is inherent in most jobs. Maybe arriving a little early would permit you to pace yourself better. Maybe a plant, poster, or other item would help to individualize your workspace, and other kinds of equipment—corkboard walls, for example—would enable you to function more effectively.

3. *Take the creative approach to problem solving.* Creative people usually recognize each problem as an opportunity. Problem solving begins with defining the problem. To discover innovative solutions, ask questions; turn the problem upside down; consider a new approach to old roadblocks. The results may surprise you.

4. *Associate with other creative people.* They're most apt to appreciate you and nurture your originality. With them you're more free to express yourself. They'll counter your ideas with theories of their own. Most of us can produce better ideas if we're teamed with the right partner.

5. *Express your willingness to participate in creative assignments.* Identify creative individuals, organize brainstorming teams, and dramatize problems requiring creative solutions. If your company is receptive, opportunities for more creative assignments may be in the offing.

6. *Identify supervisors and management team members who are receptive to creative ideas.* Other creative individuals usually are. Becoming involved with them on committees and projects allows you to bounce ideas off each other. If you're compatible with them, they may help you sell your ideas.

7. *Be creative about presenting your ideas.* To be successful, you may have to develop a strategy. Stressing their benefits to all tends to depersonalize your ideas; thus, it lowers resistance. With traditionalists, who view "change" as a threat the term "modify" is more acceptable.

8. *Through your employee organization or union encourage management to set a higher value on worthwhile ideas.* Good ideas can solve nagging problems, get crucial projects off to a good start, cut costs, and the like. They should be rewarded with recognition and cash incentives.

9. *Remember that creativity flourishes in a nurturing environment.* The right environment is usually characterized by psychological freedom and individual recognition. If you change jobs, this could be a consideration. Listing the right environment among your priorities could win you a job that's thoroughly stimulating and fulfilling.

10. *Foster your creativity off the job.* Your personal life contains more options than your work life. There are jobs that just don't lend themselves to a creative approach as well as supervisors who just aren't receptive. One way of dealing with the resulting frustrations is to exercise your creativity at home. Creative hobbies and avocations are available to everyone, including the severely handicapped. Many local organizations exist in which creative people get together, such as camera clubs; and schools are another place to sharpen your abilities. Increasing your perceptions and intuition in such ways will make you a more valuable employee when the creative job opportunity *does* come your way.

Creativity is too big and complex a subject to cover easily; one good way to learn how to understand and handle your own abilities is to read about the creative process.

Concentration Works Like a Charm

You've been in this situation before. You're sitting at your desk trying to read an important document, or you're working on a report that's due at the end of the day. But your telephone keeps ringing every five minutes and the people next to you are having a loud conversation; or the hum of the photocopying machine is distracting you.

If you're lucky enough to have a private office, you merely shut the door and take the phone off the hook until you've finished your work. But what if your office is shared? Suppose your work area is merely a desk or module in a vast area teeming with activity? What if there's no door you can close?

If that's the case, then you may have to teach yourself to concentrate on what you're doing and tune out your outside environment. If you learn how to concentrate, you'll probably be able to accomplish significantly more work than you could have ever believed possible.

The ability to concentrate varies from one individual to another. Some people learned at an early age. Peggy, a bookworm, had to concentrate if she wanted to read. With five sisters and brothers, the house was rarely quiet; privacy was unheard of. If concentration is difficult for you, the problem could be that you haven't developed your skill. Randy could never concentrate. Now an accountant, he participated in a company-sponsored seminar and mastered the technique.

Like tennis, however, concentration isn't something you'll master overnight. Understanding the concept makes it easier. Practice helps. A strong desire enables you to progress more rapidly. To get you started, here are some techniques gleaned from psychologists, time-management consultants, and other sources:

1.   *Understand what concentration is and what it isn't.* Concentration isn't an isolated property like the sense of smell. Instead, it's a skill which can be learned.

2.   *Practice with relatively short periods of concentration.* Discover how long your attention span is and work from there.

3.   *Build concentration time gradually.* From five minutes work your way to seven, ten, fifteen, and finally twenty. A reasonable goal for most people is to be able to concentrate from thirty to forty minutes.

4.   *Try to minimize external interruptions.* When you need to concentrate, try to create the right environment. Ask someone else to answer the phone. Hang a sign in your work area proclaiming, "quiet time."

5.   *Avoid interrupting yourself.* When we're bored, we tend to create distractions for a change of pace. That may explain the sudden thirst or urgent need to call someone. Recognizing the problem, you'll manage it better.

6.   *Set your mind to do it.* The more you focus your attention on what you're doing, the more effective you become in performing the task at hand.

7.   *Clear your desk.* How can you concentrate with ten piles of work staring you in the face . . . and possibly threatening to topple over? If orderly piles are part of your priority system, put them on another desk.

8.   *Find yourself a hideaway.* For certain types of assignments, remove yourself to an isolated place, perhaps an office belonging to someone who's out of town.

9.   *Work with pencil in hand.* Having a pencil ready helps you avoid distracting delays and encourages note taking, a useful habit.

10.   *Learn to use a highlighter.* Transparent markers are an underutilized resource. Highlighting topic sentences, key passages in company manuals, and parts of catalogs makes quick referral a breeze.

11.   *Respect your natural energy cycles.* Your energy isn't constant. Discovering your best concentration times and planning around them could increase your productivity as much as twenty-five percent.

12. *Increase self-discipline.* Ever notice how some people can plug themselves in and accomplish virtually any goal they set for themselves? Their secret is self-discipline. You can acquire it, too.

13. *In setting deadlines, compete with your own best time.* With tasks you do often, time your performance, record the time, and try to improve it.

14. *Make it easy to get back into a task after interruptions by ending on a high note.* With writer's block always staring them in the face, writers learn to leave work in mid-sentence or at some point that makes it easy to retrieve the thread.

15. *Capitalize on methods that work for you.* Some people need tight deadlines. Others demand a high level of motivation. Learning what works for you is half the battle.

16. *Don't interfere with others' concentration.* Learning to concentrate will increase your respect for others' efforts. Some interruptions can wait; you'll know which ones they are.

How's Your Working-Time Productivity?

How many hours a week do you work?

The answer you're likely to give is the number of hours agreed upon when your organization hired you . . . be they forty hours, thirty-five, or whatever. But when you stop to think, those figures simply mean the amount of time you're at your work place, not the time actually spent in productive work.

We see many cartoons about people hanging around the water cooler or Coke machine; we hear jokes about marathon coffee breaks that cause employers to implore their people to take a few "work breaks" as well. And certainly you see gab sessions going on where you work, people performing personal business, and so on—all in addition to scheduled breaks. Nobody except the company apparently takes this kind of behavior seriously.

A new study suggests that this on-the-job, nonworking behavior is seriously cutting into already worrisome productivity problems. It also provides some surprising information about who does most of the "goofing-off" at work; it brings to the surface pay and training differentials.

Who Takes the Most on-the-Job Breaks? Two University of Michigan researchers, Frank Stafford and Greg Duncan, developed a method of measuring the time people spend in scheduled breaks, as well as in talking to friends, doing personal business, or just relaxing.

When they put their measuring method to work in various organizations, it showed that the average, employed male worker spends approximately fifty-two minutes, or eleven percent, of working time each day in nonwork activities—scheduled and unscheduled. By contrast, the average female worker spends just thirty-five minutes, or eight percent, of the day in scheduled and nonscheduled breaks from work. The study deals a blow to the old image of women at work spending a great deal of their time repairing makeup, calling friends, and socializing.

The researchers investigated nonproductive time on the job further to determine what types of workers spend most time in either formal or informal work breaks. The results: Crafts workers, operatives, married men, and people who have less than a high school education lead the break parade.

Who Works Harder?   "Aha," you say, if you happen to be a male. "Perhaps I do take a little more time off from the job; but when I do work, I work harder to make up for it." Sorry, but it apparently isn't so, not for most male workers anyway. If you're a woman, and a male coworker gives you the "I work harder" line, you can also cite the study's finding that not only do women spend less time at work in nonwork activities, but they work harder while at work. A "work-effort scale" used in the research reveals that the effort given a job by women is 112 percent of that given by men. When education, years of experience, and total yearly work hours are taken into consideration, the figure increased to 115 percent.

Unmarried women scored the highest on the work-effort scale and accounted for the least amount of nonwork time. Married men scored slightly higher than unmarried men on the effort index, but they also took more break time.

Who expends the greatest effort per hours at work? A very interesting group emerges from this study. The professional, the union member, and the part-time worker are in this hardest working category.

Pay and Training Factors   The University of Michigan study raises the question of whether hard work really pays. The data suggest that the average working man makes $7.00 per hour on the job and the average working woman only $4.34. Yet, when their respective work hours are adjusted to account for the amount of total break time and time spent for on-the-job training, these wage rates become $8.48 for men and $4.86 for women.

On-the-job training continues to be an important factor in work the researchers report: About sixty percent of the individuals studied report receiving some type of training. As might be expected, more young people—about seventy-five percent of those under twenty-five—get such training, as compared with about twenty-five percent of the fifty-five to sixty-four age group. Interestingly, the more education you have, the more likely you are to receive on-the-job training; people with some college or junior college background get more training than those with less than a high school education.

Who Commutes Most? Commuting is another area of nonproductive use of time in relation to work in the researchers' view; so they investigated the time involved. Conclusion: The average married man spends 253 minutes a week in this travel, whereas the married woman averages only 178 minutes a week.

What Does All This Mean? The study underlines the growing concern of business with productivity on the job. With operating costs climbing steadily . . . in energy, supplies, working space, and wages, it is fast becoming a matter of survival for companies to be sure that productivity is in balance with salary outlay.

Productivity is a pressing concern in our nation's economy today. Current thinking about compensation is to give raises on the basis of superior performance. At the same time, social pressures for equality of wages between men and women are getting a boost from findings such as these. It's a good time to make sure your WCQ (Water Cooler Quotient) doesn't work against you.

Knowing How to Listen Makes You a Valued Employee

A large manufacturing firm has instituted a multimillion dollar advertising campaign that asks you to listen, not to buy.

Sperry Corporation's, "We understand how important it is to listen" campaign is a public proclamation of a message being given to its 90,000 U.S. and overseas employees with its listening-instruction program.

Why is a company that is known for its computers, farm equipment, and flight controls interested in increasing our awareness about listening? "Inefficient and ineffective listening is extremely costly," says the booklet prepared by the company to explain its campaign. "With more than 100 million workers in America, a simple ten-dollar listening mistake by each of them would cost a billion dollars."

How can "not listening" be expensive? A secretary who fails to listen to instructions may complete a time-consuming typing assignment on the wrong kind of paper. A mechanic who fails to listen to the car owner's complaints may overlook the key problem in the car he's repairing. A salesperson who does not listen to the customer may fail to present the merchandise most useful to the buyer's needs and end up with no sale or a smaller one than he could sell.

"Knowing how to listen could double the efficiency of American business. Did you hear that?" says the headline of one of Sperry's ads, which goes on to say that most business people spend half of their work-day listening but that this is done at only a 25 percent efficiency level.

What is listening? Sperry gives a broader definition than the dictionary's "Making a conscious effort to hear." Hearing is just the "physical part," says Sperry. Equally important are interpretation of what was heard, evaluating the information, and reaction based on what you have heard and evaluated.

Among the poor listening habits Sperry claims many of us have are letting emotion-laden words arouse personal antagonism, allowing distractions to interfere with listening, and criticizing the speaker's delivery or mannerisms. Some less obvious mistakes include listening primarily for facts (Sperry wants us to listen for ideas and central themes), judging the speaker before you've understood what he's said, and resisting listening to difficult material.

Daydreaming is another potential hazard to good listening. The opportunity for this kind of distraction from listening is created because people speak at a rate of 100 to 200 words per minute, but people think at a rate of 600 to 800 words per minute. Try using this time effectively. Think about what the speaker has been saying or where the speaker is going.

Listening carefully to get the real meaning of what a person is saying is a technique included in training lecturers at a major weight control organization. "If a person asks, 'Can I eat caraway seeds?' you have to listen carefully to learn that the person really wants to have cream cheese on rye bread," said a training representative. Listening to a person's tone of voice and watching body language are two clues to better understanding of what a person is saying, noted the trainer.

Sperry notes that of our four basic communication skills—listening, speaking, reading, and writing, we spend the most time listening; and it is this skill we learn first. But of the four, the least amount of time is devoted to teaching people how to listen.

If you're convinced that listening is important, and you'd like to improve your effectiveness, where do you start? Since listening is a skill, and skills can be learned, you might start by practicing more effective listening. Here's how. Describe a lecture you've heard recently; try to recall the theme, and the arguments made to support the message. Name the subjects covered in the last newscast you listened to. List all the sounds you hear in the next fifteen minutes. With a group of people, say a word, ask the next person to repeat it, and add another word; go around the room with each person adding a word that makes sense to the developing sentence; see how long the message can be repeated without a mistake.

Sperry's program is not available to nonemployees, but a booklet describing listening skills which includes a set of quizzes to help determine your own listening ability is available without cost. Write Sperry Corporation, 1290 Avenue of the Americas, New York, NY, 10019.

Read the course descriptions of adult education programs at high schools and colleges; some already offer courses specifically aimed at better listening, while others include it with general communication skills. With the attention given to Sperry's program, more courses can be expected to be offered. Check the speech department of your local community college or university; they may be able to tell you if there are courses given in your area.

Can good listening habits help you get a job? Tests for employment should include them. No such testing is now being done, but if the cost of listening mistakes is so high, a skilled listener should be a highly valued employee.

Reading Faster for Better Job Performance

A clerk/typist in the training department, Jennifer finds her time increasingly taken up with reading. Her boss likes her to review professional journals and identify material of immediate interest. She also reviews brochures of professional seminars. With piles of incoming and outgoing reports to look over, Jennifer's reading threatens to consume *all* her time.

Maybe, like Jennie, you find yourself reading more than you want to. A virtual barrage of paperwork and printed information threatens to smother everyone in the work force. Increasingly it becomes necessary to manage the reading problem before it manages you.

Fortunately, the situation isn't hopeless. Reading needn't consume that much time. You can read faster, even two or three times faster, *without reducing comprehension*.

When Jennie shared her concern with the training coordinator, he offered to send her to a speed reading class at the community college. Jennie also could have taught herself by using self-help books from the library.

By learning to read faster, you can make yourself more valuable and productive to the company for which you work. Why not start now?

Before increasing your reading speed, it will help to understand *why* so many adults read at such slow speeds of 100 to 200 words per minute. Much of the blame can be attributed to three faulty reading habits.

- *Regressing*. It's not uncommon to read a few sentences, continue, and then back up. Regressing may result from lack of confidence or concentration, poor vocabulary, or other reasons. Some readers regress as many as fifteen times for every 100 printed words. Fortunately, this problem is easy to correct.
- *Word-by-word reading*. Many second graders are careful, word-by-word readers. But you don't want to read that slowly. Like regressing, word-by-word reading is relatively easy to overcome.

- *Vocalizing.* Without knowing it, you could be plagued by this problem. To find out, place a finger on your lips. Are they moving as you read? They shouldn't be—that habit slows you down. Now place a finger on either side of your voice box on your throat as you read this article. If you discover yourself vocalizing at that level, don't be discouraged. Though not an easy habit to break, vocalizing doesn't have to slow you down.

The best way to correct these shortcomings is to *push* yourself along. A simple device called a pacer will help you gain momentum. To make a supply of pacers, use a clean manila folder. Cut as many 2 × 3-inch rectangles as you can. Put a couple in your pocket or purse; take some home; store several in your desk or work area. To complete your preparation, choose some light reading: humor, light fiction, or simple nonfiction.

Now that you've completed the preliminaries, you're ready to follow the following simple steps that have helped thousands become faster, more effective readers:

1. Use the pacer, centering it below the line you're reading. Keep it moving smoothly, but a little faster than your eyes progress in comfort. Learn to turn the card, using the wide side for long lines, the narrow side for short lines, such as the columns of a newspaper or magazine. If you still find yourself regressing, try placing the pacer *above* the printed line. At this point, don't worry about comprehension. Your eyes are learning new patterns; your brain will catch up.

2. Train your eyes to see phrases (. . . hurtling through space . . .) instead of words (. . . fast . . . readers . . . have . . . more . . . time . . . for . . . fun . . .). Your goal: to see each line at a glance.

3. Avoid vocalizing. In addition to using the pacer, it helps to be aware of this potential problem. Increasing the speed at which you move the pacer forces your eyes to speed their pace and soon defeats the vocalizing habit.

For greater gains, try regular fifteen minute-a-day practice sessions. To maintain increased reading speed, the new techniques *must* become a habit. Apply them gradually to all reading.

One other problem could be putting the brakes on your reading speed. If you're reading a few levels beyond your vocabulary, unfamiliar words tend to slow your progress. A self-help vocabulary builder can be very useful here. They are available in hard or soft cover from your bookstore or library.

Comprehension may drop at first. But gains will come with added experience and skill at the new speeds, says Professor James I. Brown of the University of Minnesota, where he conducts a popular class in speed reading.

Within a week you can be reading twice as fast as you are today. To measure your progress, find a speed reading reference that contains timed readings (the words have been counted so you can easily calculate reading speeds). Check your speed before using the pacer and again after a week of daily practice. The results will surprise you. Though most adults read at speeds of 300 words a minute, it is possible to read and comprehend 1,000 words a minute, and more.

Memory Tricks That Will Work for You on the Job

Have you ever walked into a phone booth and remembered the name of every manager in your territory but forgotten your boss's phone number? or stood up at a meeting to introduce your special guest and forgotten her name? or promised your office mate a prune danish and came up empty handed . . . because you forgot?

If you've had these or similar experiences, perhaps you've wondered how your memory works and why it sometimes lets you down. When it doesn't count, you can remember the price of every item in your sales catalog; then you stumble trying to introduce your supervisor to an important client.

Compare the memory to a giant retrieval system, and you'll find it understandable that items may be misplaced from time to time. A lot of forgetting is probably due to carelessness. We listen in a half-hearted manner and then wonder why we don't remember. However, some forgetting is intentional. We repress memories or thoughts that trigger unpleasant sensations, such as jealousy or fear. Someone who failed a particularly difficult course like calculus may insulate himself or herself against pain by forgetting the episode entirely. Research indicates we remember and forget selectively. What you don't care to hear, you probably don't remember. Also, distractions and stress sometimes prevent our storing information for later retrieval.

One of the most irritating situations occurs around "tip-of-the-tongue" retrieval. It's probably happened to you. Trying to recall a certain word or idea, you couldn't quite grasp it. Chances are that this memory failure happens at the most inconvenient times.

Here are some suggestions designed to help you remember. A good memory increases your value as an employee. Your coworkers and superiors will turn to you to help them with their jobs because *you'll* remember where everything is, the name of an important client's secretary, and what day that big sales letter was mailed.

1. *Write things down.* Trusting your memory is neither businesslike nor particularly smart. Making notes on a pad frees you to remember other, more important information and relieves you of the hassles that occur when messages are forgotten.

2. *Develop a system for organizing messages.* Lost messages don't help anyone very much. To prevent losing them, put them on a bulletin board. Placed near the phone, messages are convenient to all. Or you could file them in a folder, organized by the date on which you're supposed to act on them.

3. *Be conscious of what you want to remember.* Being alert, you make a conscious effort to listen and remember, for example, people's names . . . or how to use a certain piece of machinery on which you'll be working.

4. *Repeat to remember longer.* Have you ever needed to remember a phone number when you didn't have a pencil? Repetition probably helped. When she was learning how to handle purchase orders, ambitious Lynn repeated the procedure to herself very often. Her supervisor was surprised that she mastered the new assignment so quickly.

5. *Look beneath the surface at what the information means.* It helps to see information in relation to other information, to define terms, to analyze figures, and so forth. Mnemonic devices, such as the ones you learned in school ("*i* before *e* except after *c*" . . . "thirty days has September . . ."), are useful. You might remember Mr. Greene's name because he always wears a green tie. Discover which memory tricks work best for you.

6. *Spread memory work out over several sessions.* Were you asked to give a speech at the retirement party? Are you trying to learn speedwriting to increase productivity? Divide the task into segments and schedule a session each day. You'll be surprised how much easier the task becomes.

7. *Organize material for better recall.* For best results, organize dates into a time sequence, numerals by number of digits, and information chronologically or by department or function. This method works particularly well for classifying categories of equipment, merchandise, and the like for inventory.

8. *Use physical reminders to trigger your memory.* It helps to use a physical clue: a chair in the doorway, a sign on the inside of the window, storeroom keys tied to your waist. One psychologist describes a professional woman who had a hard time remembering to replay the tape on her telephone answering device. Her trick? Placing her keys on the device when she entered the room, which reminded her to play back the day's messages. Picking them up became the signal for making the device operative when she went out again.

9. *When remembering is impossible, jot down the information and keep it handy.* Zip codes pose a special problem for Nancy. When callers ask about zip codes for company franchises, she refers to a list taped to her desk near the phone. Laura does the same with hard-to-spell words.

Parallel always gives her trouble. Instead of going to the dictionary every time, she jotted down the information and taped it to her typewriter stand. For Ted it's the prices of fast-selling parts. They're taped in the front of his order pad to save him time every working day.

Business Etiquette: Changing Rules

A coworker took you to lunch on your birthday. Should you reciprocate?

If a female and male business associate are walking into a building together, is it correct for the woman to open the door if she gets there first?

As a woman moving into sales management, you feel confident about everything except entertaining the occasional male client(s) at lunch or dinner. Is there a discreet way to handle the check?

If you're into a career, you've probably encountered situations similar to these. You've wondered when to turn to an etiquette book and when to operate on the basis of what *feels* right. The news is that many career people are discovering new freedom where manners are concerned. Virtually any behavior that feels appropriate to you and demonstrates your concern for others is acceptable in today's business environment. For special problems you can still turn to the answer people.

Many of your coworkers started their jobs in a highly authoritarian environment. That their behavior still carries strong overtones of that era shouldn't surprise you. They addressed the boss as "Mister" and "sir"; to do otherwise was unthinkable. Upper management was treated with almost ceremonial deference. The same strict code produced stilted letters and mechanical memos, but the fine points of business etiquette were strictly observed.

Along with technology, social values, and employees' rights, good manners have undergone a dramatic transition in recent years. Today's horizons are broader; authoritarianism has declined.

But some things *never* go out of style. Saying "please" and "thank you" promptly and often still keeps the wheels oiled and running smoothly. Demonstrating a willingness to cooperate is an essential business rule. Borrowing from others without their permission is a no-no. Cleaning up your own coffee cups and potential litter is as fundamental as keeping to the right lane while driving. Treating people as you'd like to be treated makes you No. 1 with coworkers, clients, and customers.

To clarify some of the thorny questions career people face, *Employment World* consulted several authoritative sources. Here are some of the questions workers have been asking, along with some of the answers:

"Why is business etiquette so important?"

Though you may care little for social amenities and less about how others perceive your behavior, the degree to which you practice etiquette and courtesy does affect your image. If upward mobility figures in your plans, that image is something you can ill afford to damage.

Playing by the rules is a career plus, particularly when it comes to being assigned promotions, new clients, or projects. First to be tapped are those who handle themselves appropriately in difficult situations.

"How I act is my own affair—isn't it?"

Maybe; maybe not. Courtesy expresses your concern for others; it demonstrates the *quality* of your concern. To carry the idea a step further, let's take a look at Carol. An avid environmentalist, she'd be outraged if her office mate smoked in their shared quarters. Carol, however, enjoys music and keeps a radio on her desk. When she turns it on, Carol is negligent about asking, "Do you mind?" Jean, on the other hand, is bothered by noise pollution and wishes she could say *no* without damaging the relationship.

"I'm busy. Doesn't courtesy take a lot of extra time?"

Saying "please" and "thanks" takes only a second or two. Stopping to listen when someone wants to talk; waiting for a coworker to reach a stopping place, rather than interrupting; helping an overloaded file clerk reach his or her destination safely—some acts of courtesy *do* take a little longer. The other side of the coin is that returning calls promptly helps you avoid interruptions later; taking time to clarify your instructions via feedback prevents misunderstandings and sometimes major hassles, too. In the long run courtesy probably *saves* time, as well as wear and tear.

"What about women and shaking hands?"

A pleasant way of breaking the ice, handshaking is appropriate in many situations. According to etiquette expert Elizabeth Post, "Businesswomen should act the same way that businessmen would. If clients or customers come into their offices, both men and women should rise and shake hands."

"Isn't business courtesy a maze of thou-shalt-nots?"

Not necessarily. For example, overstaying appointments; repairing makeup, manicuring, or chewing gum while on duty; putting one's feet on the desk or removing shoes; casual chatting during working hours; and keeping a cluttered desk are obvious no-no's.

"And doors . . . who opens them for whom?"

"Whoever happens to be in the lead opens the door and holds it for the other," Baldridge suggests. "Whoever first sees the taxi hails it." In an equal world, the general operating principles are efficiency, kindness, and elementary good sense.

As a woman who takes a male client to lunch, you make it clear when you invite him that it is the company's invitation and will go on your expense account. Another suggestion is to tell the waiter you want the bill given to you.

A birthday lunch needn't be a dilemma, either. Here is a classic opportunity to do what makes you feel good. If you want to reciprocate for a lunch treat, you have a lot of options: a gift, a plant, or an invitation to your home.

In many ways business etiquette closely resembles social etiquette: courtesy, concern for others, and common sense are what usually dictate the rules. If you're already practicing them in your personal life, there will be no problem applying them to your professional life.

2

Your Personality and Work

How often have you thought, "If *they*'d just let me alone, I could get this job done?" But *they*—coworkers, your boss, even that nagging voice in the back of your head telling you what you *should* have done—won't stop you know. People problems are inherent in any job. A disagreement with your boss, shyness, or being unable to stand up for yourself can lower your efficiency just as surely as broken-down equipment or inadequate support staff.

"Personality problems" are one of those aspects of work that people are most frightened by—assertiveness, for example. A library of books, lecture notes, articles, and videotapes have explained the difference between assertiveness and aggressiveness; yet some people still are afraid to stand-up and protect their own interests. Or think about attitude. At some time during your life, someone—maybe a kindergarten teacher, an army sergeant, or a boss—has told you, "I don't like your attitude." What *is* a good work attitude, and how do you get one?

Most important of the people skills that today's jobs require is the ability to get across to bosses and coworkers the message you want to project about yourself. Without bragging or undue modesty, you want them to know that you're bright, hard-working, responsible, *and* on your way up.

You can probably remember more than one incident when you've felt pushed around on the job. Possibly a boss asked you to stay late one night because he or she knew you wouldn't mind. Usually you wouldn't mind; but you had a dinner engagement that night and cancelled it because you didn't know how to say "no" to the boss.

Or it might have been a coworker who asked you to cover for her while she took an extra long lunch. You were burning inside because you had to work through lunch that day; but you agreed to do it because you couldn't bring yourself to say no.

If you've ever been in situations like these, you have good reason to question whether you're assertive enough. Assertiveness is perhaps one of the most important skills you can learn on the job. With it, you'll be able to get what *you* want without putting your coworkers and supervisors off; without assertiveness you may find yourself being taken advantage of.

To help you say no and cope with other job problems, you may want to consider reading one of a number of books or taking a course on assertiveness training. In the meantime here are some easy-to-learn and effective assertiveness techniques.

1. *The assertive response to criticism* is based on agreement. Basically, you agree with any truth or general logic in the critic's remarks. Suppose your supervisor asks for a conference. "Lynn," he remarks, "you're taking longer to process the purchase orders." By agreeing ("Perhaps you're right." or "You may have a point there."), you block further criticism. To pursue the subject, the supervisor must resort to a more rational approach ("Is there something we can do about it?").

2. *Workable compromise* enables you to suggest alternatives to existing practices. Suppose your four-member car pool is set up so that members take turns driving but on an irregular basis. This system makes it hard for your family to know in advance when they can use the car; your only alternative is the bus, which is slower and not as much fun. You'd prefer to drive, for example, every Tuesday and every fourth Friday. You convince your colleagues that taking turns driving on a regular schedule is workable. Your compromise earns the group's approval, and the problem is solved.

3. *Broken record* refers to the use of calm repetition. Suppose you and Harold have signed up for the same two weeks' vacation. Harold wants to go back East for his college reunion. The boss is urging you to give in although seniority gives you first choice.

"I want the first two weeks in June," you assert.

"But, Luke, you can always . . . ," the boss begins.

"I want the first two weeks in June."

How many times must you repeat? Four or five is usually enough.

4. *Self-disclosure* is simply revealing information about yourself, that is, how you *think* and *feel*, allowing communication to flow both ways. "How's your day going?" your colleague Hal inquires over lunch. "Fine," you reply. Since Hal has indicated he wants to talk, you can disclose what you'd like to talk *about*. "But instead of talking shop, I'd like to make plans for the weekend. How about jogging with me Saturday?"

5. *Negative assertion* helps you teach others to accept your faults and errors. When someone comments on your forgetfulness, you strongly agree: "You're right. Because of my heavy workload, I do forget sometimes." Since it lines you up with the critic, negative assertion frees you of the need to apologize and allows you to assign a reason to the point criticized.

6. *Role playing* is so simple that it's used in teaching young children. Planning to ask for a raise? To handle the situation assertively requires practice for most of us. Ask a friend to play the role of boss as you act out what you'll say and how the boss will respond. Then reverse roles. You play the boss; let the friend be you. The insights you gain may surprise you.

7. *Teaching others how you want to be treated* demonstrates assertiveness at its most basic level. Many of us carry victim habits from childhood. As one psychologist notes, we must build up a strong internal nonvictim structure by continually reminding ourselves of our nonvictim status: "I am not now and never will be a victim again!" Suppose a friend or a co-worker is angry at you and doesn't tell you why. Do you keep meekly silent and wait for the anger to pass? Why not ask, "Why are you angry? If it's something I've said or done, maybe we should talk about it."

8. *Saying no without feeling guilty* is one of your basic rights. Next time the boss asks you to work overtime when you have other plans, you'll respond, "Not tonight. I've made plans." (If you feel unsure of yourself, ask a friend to role-play the situation with you, so you'll be ready when the situation occurs.) To include workable compromise, you might add, "But how about tomorrow?"

9. *Changing your mind* is normal, even healthy, as long as others are not seriously inconvenienced. Next time you feel like changing yours, go ahead and do it. There is no need to apologize, but now and then remind people that you do reserve the right to change your mind.

Assertiveness isn't a solution to life's problems, but it does offer you some new options in terms of your behavior with others. Most people who practice assertiveness feel they've become more effective in their careers.

If you're interested in taking an assertiveness training course, check with some of the continuing education programs in your area. Many offer low-cost seminars.

How to Maintain a Good Work Attitude

Richard Osk began work as a copy boy at the *New York Herald Tribune* the same day in 1927 that Charles Lindbergh landed the "Spirit of St. Louis" in Paris. The newsroom was electrified. The librarian said to Osk, "Isn't it exciting?"

"Oh, yes, ma'am," he answered thinking she was talking about Richard's first day at work.

Richard Osk had a good attitude about work. The excitement of just being in that newsroom transcended, for him, Lindbergh's achievement. Now retired from newspaper work and living in Florida, Richard Osk retains this "Isn't it exciting?" attitude for each day.

The person who brings a positive attitude to a job has a better chance of climbing up the ladder and will likely perform more efficiently than will persons with negative or mediocre attitudes. While some workers, by their nature and experience, have better attitudes than others, good attitudes can be cultivated.

First, take pencil in hand and list the positive aspects of your job. Don't forget such items as opportunities for promotion, benefits, and coworkers, as well as free parking, proximity to home, and training opportunities.

Next, analyze your career goals. List the progress you have made since this time last year. Don't forget any raise you have had, new and more efficient tools furnished, or better working conditions provided.

Finally, list the people you have contact with on a daily basis at work. Beside each name write a phrase describing this person's greatest strength. For example: "Jim—helpfulness and patience; Gene—sense of humor; Mark—concern for his family; Evelyn—training ability."

Exercises such as these will help you understand your job and its benefits and will help you understand your coworkers and appreciate them. Understanding will help improve your work attitude.

Maurice Frasier, training manager for Motorola in Austin, Texas, recollects that one of the first training sessions requested when she took her present job was teaching people how to treat other people.

"What do you mean?" she asked the supervisor making the request.

"Well," he said, "we need to know how to reject a piece of work or an idea without rejecting the person doing the work or offering the idea. We need to know how to generate a good attitude toward others."

"You mean the Golden Rule?"

"That's it," he answered.

The resulting training session stressed ways to improve attitudes. Good attitudes are not generated by acceptance of shoddy work, but correction should be given between two slices of praise—like a sandwich. For example: "You work rapidly and your production is high. However, if you slowed down a bit, you wouldn't have to re-do so much. We value your enthusiasm."

Cultivating good listening skills helps morale and attitudes. If you *hear* and *understand* directions from your supervisor, you will do a more creditable job and receive praise for your work, and your attitudes will improve. If you see a change that could help improve efficiency, you should make the suggestion to the supervisor in a positive, non-threatening manner.

Making yourself heard and understood is also important to maintaining good attitudes. Here are some effective ways of holding someone's attention.

- Start with a conclusion, never with a question. (Instead of asking your boss, "Why don't you . . . ?", say to him "I believe we can cut down absenteeism if. . . .")
- Get to your main idea quickly. Otherwise, by the time you finally make your point, your listener's mind may have skipped ahead of what you're saying.
- Talk in terms of potential benefits to the listener whenever possible. People will take interest if what you say concerns them. By all means be as specific as you can and avoid generalities.

Barbara Walters, asked who is the sexiest man she has ever interviewed, answered, "President Carter." She explained that of all the men she has talked with, he *listened*—he gave his complete attention to the interview and the interviewer.

This attitude of listening, of paying attention, is one that will increase the understanding of fellow workers, as well as of supervisors and the instructions they give.

Listening is not easy—it calls for intense application; but you'll find that the rewards are worth the effort.

A sense of humor is both good medicine and an indicator of good attitudes. He who laughs at himself—not at others—will always have friends and boosters. A sense of humor can be nurtured to improve attitudes.

Shared laughter sets a pattern of good attitudes, as well as a feeling of camaraderie.

How to Deal with Shyness at Work

One of the problems of shyness is that it tends to be self-perpetuating. People who are shy tend to stay in the background, draw little attention to themselves, seldom initiate conversations, submit ideas, or take strong actions of any kind. This is as neat a formula as can be devised for getting absolutely nowhere in today's hustling and competitive working world.

Shyness is not only a major obstacle to getting ahead in the world of work, it's a painful burden for people who suffer from it. They are losing some of the nicer benefits of working—the pleasant give-and-take among people working together, the active feeling of being part of a team accomplishing a task, and the group socializing that occurs on company ski trips, bowling nights, or weekend excursions. Because speaking up on their own behalf is very difficult for shy people, they tend to be left out or bypassed when praises or raises go around. Moreover, having painfully established a niche in the organization, many suffering from this problem are reluctant to make a change, that is, to apply for the more interesting jobs in the company's job-posting program or to take training that will lead to new kinds of work.

Looking for a new job and going through a variety of interviews and tests among strange people is hard enough for anyone. But it's definitely one of the most severe tests that shy people encounter.

While we can't resolve the whole problem of the shy personality in a page or two, we can certainly make some suggestions that may help a shy person to handle everyday problems in the workplace.

How can you overcome shyness on the job? Good communications skills are the answer. Start conversations. Take an interest in the person you're talking to or what's going on in the company. You'll find that if you get involved with other people, your shyness will disappear.

But how do you get involved with other people? Invite your fellow workers to lunch, dinner, or even a coffee break. Show interest in co-workers' jobs by asking questions. Think of ways you can invite a conversation. Do a lot of smiling. You can actually *practice* friendliness. (And don't forget to use these techniques away from the office—with people in stores or other places.)

How do you cope with job interviews? If you are shy and preparing for an interview, it would be wise to do research on the company you hope will hire you. Make a list of questions you think you'll be asked and try answering them. You might use a tape recorder or even act out the interview with a friend. While preparing for your interview, by all means think positively about yourself. Rehearse your accomplishments; accent the positive. After all, an interview *is* a sales situation; don't be afraid that you're bragging.

It might help you, when getting ready for an interview, to bring along a written check list. Let the employer see you've done your homework. Use it to help yourself ask questions that relate to the job or the company.

Never forget that good communication is the key for a meaningful dialogue. All right, you can't help being shy, perhaps. But you can—and you should—take steps to handle it, especially in the work situation.

How to Have a Confrontation at Work

It's nice to be nice, but on the job it's even more important to be effective. Sometimes, in order to do the job, you will have to disagree, criticize, or talk back to people. Deliberately planning a confrontation may seem frightening, but experts in business communications say you should *plan* these communication events, not just let them happen.

One of the keys to not having a discussion escalate into a shouting match is to express your feelings before they reach the boiling point. Another key is to know how to express these feelings in ways that other people find acceptable. However, most people don't know how to disagree without being disagreeable.

It can be done. For the next time you need to confront someone at work, here are ten tips from the experts that will help your planning:

1. Decide if a discussion is really necessary. What will you gain? What do you stand to lose if you say nothing? If you have a complaint, have some definite action in mind that you want the other person to take to resolve the problem. Try to conclude (not begin) your discussion with this suggestion. Put yourself in the other person's shoes. Why, from their point of view, should he/she want to do this? Try to understand their reasons for wanting to do this, not just your reasons for wanting it done.

2. Pick your time and place carefully. For example, if you need to speak to your boss and he/she is not a morning person, don't rush in at 8:30 A.M. before morning coffee. Pick a time when the other person is most likely to be receptive. If the topic is a sensitive one, choose a place where others can't overhear. If the time you ask for isn't convenient, be ready to negotiate a mutually acceptable time and place.

3. Give the other person clear verbal clues before launching into your subject. Say, "There's something I'd like to talk about. Can you spare me about ten minutes to discuss . . . ?" This clue gives the other person the opportunity to tune into what you're thinking and decide to discuss it now or arrange a time and place that's more convenient.

4. Begin on a positive note, something you can agree on, before going on to disagree. If you have to criticize, try to find something the other person did that you can sincerely compliment.

5. Make "I" statements; not "you" statements. "I misunderstood" is a lot easier for the other person to take than "You didn't explain this clearly," even if the fault is theirs. "I" statements reveal how you feel. "You" statements are usually accusations which put the other person on the defensive. Once they start defending themselves, they will stop listening to what you have to say. It's better to say, "I felt humiliated at the meeting," not "You're always putting me down." You're trying to get a message across, not starting a debate about character.

6. Stick to your main point and avoid side issues and personalities. Stay in the present and future rather than bring-up things this person has done to annoy you in the past. Confine your discussion to something specific this person has done or not done. Don't be sidetracked into personalities. Don't call them "incompetent," because it won't help; but discussing something done that was incompetent could help them to change.

7. State what you have to say as briefly and specifically as possible. "You're never on time" is vague. The statement, "You were late Monday, Tuesday, Thursday, and Friday last week," is specific. "You don't appreciate what I do" is a vague, as well as a "you," type of statement. "I'd like you to give me more positive feedback" is a specific "I" type of statement.

8. Use diplomatic language. Courtesy and tact are signs of strength, not weakness. Say, "I think you've made a mistake," not, "You're wrong!" and, "Please let me finish what I'm saying," not, "Stop interrupting!" Even if the other person is rude, overbearing, and obnoxious, do not reply in kind, it will gain nothing and could lose you the opportunity to have your say.

9. Watch your tone of voice. Other persons will react more to the tone of what you have to say than to your actual words. If they become defensive and angry for no apparent reason, it may be a reaction to your angry, sarcastic, or sneering tone. If they brush you off without a hearing, they may be reacting to a timid or tentative tone in your voice that sounds like you don't really mean what you say. If necessary, practice what you will say with a friend or with a tape recorder until you can deliver your message in a calm, even, assertive tone.

10. Finally, listen; don't just talk. Watch for nonverbal, as well as verbal, clues to how other people react to your message. Give them time to respond, and be ready to adjust what you say in return.

Most people avoid confrontations at work, as well as in their personal lives, because they fear losing. But not all confrontations are win/lose. There are also win/win situations. In fact, in the ideal negotiation each side feels it has gained. If, instead of a "you against me" feeling, you can create an atmosphere of "us" against the problem, both of you will gain from the confrontation.

Dealing with a Difficult Boss

You, like most employees, have conflicts or differences of opinion with your boss from time to time. Perhaps it is a simple matter of being criticized or corrected. The correction may be warranted, even helpful. The criticism may hurt . . . and be true. Sometimes, however, it is a more serious conflict and cannot be resolved without leaving one of you angry and resentful. For instance: Have you risen up in wrath after working hard on another assigned project and being told again by the boss that it wasn't what he had asked you for? Have you sulked when your pet idea was rejected as stupid? After the boss told you it was your job to make coffee every morning, even though you don't drink coffee yourself, did you refuse, saying it wasn't part of your job?

In situations like these, when you and your boss are at odds, you had better examine the situation as openly and as dispassionately as possible and try to come up with some solution you can live with.

Five steps that you can take in dealing with a serious conflict are as follows:

1. Defuse the situation; shouting and anger do not lead to rational thought and behavior.

2. Determine the actual problem by focusing on the facts.

3. Discuss the problem and make clear-cut resolutions aimed at solving it.

4. Work at solving the problem.

5. Discuss your resolutions with your boss.

One common source of conflict between employer and employee is the boss's style of criticism. He or she should understand that it is very important to criticize a particular action and not the person who did it. For instance, if a secretary inserted the wrong data in a report, ideally a boss should say, "You made a bad mistake," and indicate exactly what the error was. The boss should not say, "Dammit, look at this report! You're stupid and you're careless!" Or, some bosses may shout and scream at you. Nobody should have to tolerate this. Name-calling, insults, and other personal remarks are also unprofessional and entirely unacceptable.

What can you do if this happens? Never respond in a similar way! You are escalating the conflict if you do. *Always defuse the situation.* If necessary, leave the boss's office, go to the rest room and compose yourself, or take a walk around the block. When you return, *determine the actual problem by focusing on the facts of the situation.* Tell your boss that it wasn't the criticism that bothered you but the language or shouting or whatever that upset you. Your boss will probably apologize.

Suppose, though, that this sort of incident is a daily or nearly daily occurrence. Your boss's style is to blow up and yell. Some bosses don't feel it is their obligation to apologize to employees. You are going to have to decide whether or not you are willing and able to put up with your boss's abrasive ways, whatever they happen to be.

The key, then, in a continuing personality conflict is to focus on the facts. First, try to determine what the problem really is. Is the boss continually criticizing your work? Does he/she get upset when you make or receive personal telephone calls? Is there any truth in what your boss is saying? Step back from the inflamed situation. Put yourself in his/her shoes. There probably is some truth involved. If so, is there anything you can do about it? If the problem is a question of the quality of your work, then you certainly can and should make every effort to improve this aspect of your performance. If the problem is more abstract, that is, if your boss says you're uncooperative or lazy or that you have a bad attitude, then you have to return to the step of focusing on the facts.

Sit down with your boss and calmly discuss the situation. Don't get angry if he/she refuses to acknowledge any inappropriate behavior on his/her part. Listen to him/her.

The purpose of this meeting is to make concrete resolutions based on fact. A sincere effort to change and improve should then follow. Set a date with your boss to review the situation. Don't expect your boss to change. He/she probably feels no obligation to do so.

What happens if you've carefully examined your part in the conflict, you've had a confrontation with your boss, you've made a sincere effort to resolve the problem, and you and your boss still aren't getting along?

Remember, time is a great resolver of conflicts. If your boss is going on a business trip, welcome it as an opportunity for everybody to cool off and regain perspective. Better yet, if you have some vacation due you, take it. But don't brood about the situation while you're walking on the beach.

The worst thing you can do is to complain to coworkers about the problem. Criticizing your boss behind his/her back is bad form. It is reasonable, however, if you feel that your boss is in the wrong, to seek assistance. Go to the Personnel Department and tell them your problem. You may learn that your boss has required a new assistant every year. "It's just his/her way," they may tell you. Nothing you do will change an abrasive, unpleasant personality.

Sometimes a basic personality conflict exists between two people, one that makes working together impossible. The conflict may not have anything to do with the quality of each other's work, or the way the work is done, or anything that involves the job at all.

When the chips are down, you are not in a position of power in this situation. The answer then is simply to request a transfer or quit. You should speak courteously to your boss before leaving, because he/she still has the power to give you a bad reference. Say something such as, "Look, for some reason we just didn't get along. I think we're both good people and good at our jobs. I'm sorry it didn't work out." Leave on an upbeat note, if at all possible.

Making a Statement about Yourself

The image you project—your appearance, your attitude, the quality of your work, and the people with whom you associate—tells more about yourself than you probably realize. These factors not only determine how others perceive you, but how they respond to you. Sometimes the image you project cannot be changed or improved. But most of the time there's room for improvement, and improvement requires perseverance.

If those around you consistently underestimate your abilities, misunderstand your motives, or fail to recognize your achievements, the problem could be that your image fails to project who you are in a manner others understand. Several factors can get in the way.

Not realizing that others see how he *looks* before they see how he *performs*, Bart arrives at his job in not-too-neat jeans, t-shirt, and sneakers without socks. Since he's a parts man in a big automobile dealership, no one expects a pin-striped suit. On the other hand, when he hands them parts, customers sometimes inquire, "Are you sure this is right?"

Bart gets tired of questions like that, but the truth is his appearance fails to reflect his competence. If he were more careful about his clothes and grooming, he might not hear such questions so often.

Unfortunately, when we think *image*, we tend to think appearance. When she was bucking for promotion to cashier, Judy spent $20 to have her hair cut and styled. When someone else got the job, Judy was angry, hurt, and resentful—not realizing it was her work attitude, not her hairdo, that prevented her from getting the promotion.

Judy and Bart aren't all that unusual. Many workers project negative images. Maybe it's time to take a closer look at your image and how it projects *you* to others.

Some of the people you encounter every day—on the bus, at the lunch counter, or in the elevator—look you over and decide who and what you are. Admittedly it's a poor basis for evaluating others, but sometimes that's all the information available for judging. If you meet someone wearing a silk suit with her nose in the air, you may assume she's a snob. Someone who pushes through a crowd to get a better look at the parade seems inconsiderate, if not downright rude.

A reporter for a Houston newspaper observed this phenomenon and decided to check it out. After letting his beard and hair grow, Bob Meckel wore ragged clothes for his first visit to the central library. Picking a book from the shelf, he pretended to drop off to sleep with his head on the table. Within ten minutes a librarian warned him about a city ordinance against sleeping in the building. A few days later Meckel returned, shaven and wearing a three-piece suit. Though he pretended to be asleep for more than thirty minutes, he was not disturbed.

If you value competence, skills, education, and other qualities more than you do image, that's your privilege. However, if *most* of the successful people you encounter seem to be making a special effort to *look* and *act* the part, maybe "packaging" carries more weight than you think.

One's image goes more deeply than appearance. In fact, it includes everything about you that others perceive. Let's take a look at some other factors that affect how others see and respond to you.

- *Your work.* All of your work makes a statement about you, but written work may speak the loudest. Every letter you send projects your image; the same goes for memos, reports, applications and résumés, and even telephone messages you jot down hurriedly for coworkers.
- *Your attitudes.* One corporation says, "What we look for in our employees is a positive, healthy outlook." Your attitude is also reflected in your enthusiasm, loyalty, and handling of difficulties.
- *Poise.* How well do you handle yourself in awkward or sensitive situations? Poise seems to come naturally to some people, but most of us have to acquire it. If you feel a need to develop yourself in this respect, one way is to choose an appropriate role model and observe that person's conduct in different situations.
- *Your associates.* When you are making friends on the job, deliberately avoid the atmosphere of nonaccomplishment. Make friends among leaders instead of followers and among men and women for whom you have genuine respect. A good rule of thumb is to form associations at every level of the hierarchy, provided you choose individuals who stand for something worthwhile. Also, if you have coffee and lunch with the same threesome everyday, you could be missing out on other exciting and stimulating relationships, both in and out of your company.

It is not difficult to build your image. There are many signs and standards by which you can achieve positive results. And when you have developed a winning image, you'll know it; you will feel right, and others will show by their responses that they feel it, too.

Interpersonal Skills for the Eighties

The 1980's hold bright promise for the job market and the people it touches, in spite of inflation. Together with new technology, the 80's will bring new approaches to old problems, new management styles, and much needed growth in productivity. As businesses scramble after lucrative new markets, change will be the first item on the agenda. In fact, change will be so widespread that you may ask yourself if *anything* can remain the same—including your own work.

If your job involves frequent contact with others: coworkers, associates, clients, and customers, for example, the answer may be *yes*, but with qualifications.

Interpersonal skills are essential to a successful and satisfying career. Whatever your job, the ability to get along with others helps you draw every morsel of success and satisfaction from it. Maybe you're in a service industry, meeting new people, persuading them that your services are best, or in research where you might be isolated in a library or laboratory most of the day, or doing your own thing in a vast office packed with people like and unlike yourself. Wherever you are, interpersonal skills enable you to reduce stress, generate satisfying relationships, and increase your career options.

For more than forty years, Dale Carnegie's best seller, *How to Win Friends and Influence People*, has been virtually required reading for anyone wanting to master interpersonal skills. Those working in sales read it and discover that people skills count for more than product technology, persuasion, or knowing how to close. Supervisors use it to ease strained relationships, gain cooperation, and generate team spirit. Professionals in such diverse fields as law, construction, agriculture, accounting, and engineering adopted Carnegie's methods successfully.

Surprisingly, considering to what extent technology, management, and other sciences have changed and will change, Carnegie's ideas are as sound as ever. They'll serve you as well in the eighties as they served the generations before you.

The social climate, however, has changed. If you signed up for a Dale Carnegie course during the 50's, your skills may be somewhat dated. Today's literature is wrapped in more personal language. Some people, perhaps including you, find it more comfortable than traditional statements. Though strongly influenced by the Carnegie approach, today's theorists have reworked the basic ideas and made them more relevant for the 80's.

- *The big secret of dealing with people, according to Carnegie, is not to criticize or judge them.* The advice is as sound as ever, and the interim has given us Dr. Norman Vincent Peale and other advocates of positive thinking, perhaps leading today's writers to clothe their statements in more positive terms.

  Criticizing and judging tends to develop misunderstanding and intolerance. It's important to understand that tolerance of people's differences prevents distress. The trap in judging others is that it may be the first step in trying to change them. Your good intentions of helping them may easily be perceived as interference and curtailment of their freedoms. Admit the possibility that it may very well be you that needs to change in order to improve your relationships or your work environment.

- *Make other people feel important.* There is no question that employers and employees would be better off if they used more "stroking" on the job. In Transactional Analysis lingo, strokes are what people do and say in order to give others okay feelings about themselves. A compliment, a pat on the back, a special look—these are examples of good, positive strokes, better known as "warm fuzzies." Negative strokes, on the other hand, ("Don't tell me you goofed again!") are called "cold pricklies." You won't need a guidebook to know the difference. Best of all are the solid gold strokes that acknowledge one's worth as a person. It's nice to hear that someone likes you, not because of what you *did*, but just because you *are* ("Oh, Helen, seeing you is such a nice surprise!").

  Dave's been away on jury duty? "Glad you're back; we really missed you!" recognizes your worth, both as a person and as an employee.

- *Become interested in others.* Develop the ability of appreciating others. And that begins with looking for the qualities that set each person apart. You'll find that people respond more enthusiastically when you notice those things which are important to them and set them apart.

Another spot of sunshine on the interpersonal scene is the trend toward helping others grow. The movement is led by training and development specialists, but anyone can get involved. Every time you motivate co-workers to try harder, solve problems, become more productive, increase their career potential, or recognize and accept a challenge, you're giving them a boost toward self-actualization and fulfillment. The result is a natural high previously reserved for teachers and others in the helping disciplines. Since there's a payoff for the helper as well as the helpee, this trend may be the frosting on the interpersonal cake.

If you feel your own skills in dealing with people aren't as sharp as they might be, it will be worthwhile to read the books on the subject. Absorbing and practicing what they teach is a sure way to make your work more satisfying in the 80's and to speed you along your career path.

3
Handling
on-the-Job Problems

Chapter 2 provided a variety of suggestions on how to convey to coworkers and bosses the message about yourself that you want them to hear. But sometimes "personality problems" go beyond shyness, your attitude, a bossy subordinate, or a notoriously difficult boss. This chapter deals with more serious problems that include not only your attitude, but also your rights under law.

Criticism is one example. No one likes it, yet constructive criticism is one method we all can use to improve job performance. Arguments too: if we use them constructively, we can grow by means of them. But there are times when arguments go beyond simple disagreement. What do you do to prevent quarrels from escalating or to mend fences after a really bad fight on the job? Or let's assume that your stomach is tied up in knots all the time. What's causing the stress you obviously feel? Do you know what to do about it?

The vastly increased numbers of women in the workplace are creating new problems for some people: women as bosses; women as targets for harassment. Are your attitudes changing with the times? What will you do if your coworkers' aren't? What are some of your rights in the workplace?

Criticism is bound to happen—on the job and off. The most efficient worker is apt to feel its sting; and no one, regardless of ability or position, is entirely immune. Much of the criticism you hear is relatively harmless; it may even be constructive. But when you are the target, it can sting like a poisoned dart.

Perhaps you've wondered how to treat those stings. Maybe there are questions about criticism you've been wanting to ask. Hopefully, the questions that follow will parallel yours, and the answers will help you cope when criticism threatens you.

Why is criticism so painful?   Criticism hurts because it exposes information we'd prefer to keep hidden. It hurts most when it's perceived as an attack on our confidence and self-esteem.

Why is coping so important?   Monday's blues often give way to Tuesday's sunshine, but criticism doesn't go away. Knowing how to cope relieves the sting and can prevent it entirely. As Dr. Norman Vincent Peale has pointed out, very often our careers, our emotional stability and even our happiness depend on how we react.

Who's responsible for the pain associated with criticism?   Some of it must be laid at the feet of those who seek satisfaction through criticizing others; those on the receiving end share the blame. By our reactions, as well as our overreactions, we compound the problem. The pain arises less from what is said than from how it's perceived. "You're still *smoking?*" someone inquires. If the smoker doesn't take the comment seriously, it's soon forgotten. Our perceptions also determine how we respond, and some responses are very unconstructive.

What are some unconstructive types of responses?   Everyone has heard the *immediate apology* ("Oh, I'm so sorry!"). It sounds too much like an admission of guilt. Another is the *defensive posture* ("Well, at least I tried!"), which can lead to arguments. The *frozen silence* may signify deep and lasting pain. Finally there is the *comment reflecting lowered self-esteem* ("I never do anything right!").

What's behind these unconstructive responses?   How people criticize and respond is usually determined by patterns developed in childhood. In some families criticism is used as a coping device. Also, most of us respond automatically, rather than rationally.

How can I assess my responses?   Take a moment to recall the last three incidents in which you faced criticism. Was your response emotional, predictable, or rational? Perhaps you handle some types of criticism rationally but allow others to trigger an emotional response. For example, working mothers often feel threatened when their parenting role is criticized.

Do some people cope better than others?   Of course. Stronger individuals are less apt to feel threatened. Students of assertiveness training develop new attitudes toward criticism, along with better coping skills.

Next time criticism comes my way, what should I do?   Keep your cool. If you have the habit of responding emotionally, it won't be easy to change. To practice the calm response, try role-playing with family and friends. Also, when you can anticipate criticism, it's easier to be in control.

Let's say I can keep my cool. What else should I do?   Take a moment to evaluate both criticism and critic. Advocates of assertiveness training distinguish between *truths* that others tell you about your behavior ("Your production is down for the third straight week.") and *opinions* they tack on ("You're not trying, are you?"). In assertiveness training, the emphasis is on listening calmly and responding to whatever *truth* the criticism contains.

Also take a look at your critic. Is it someone whose opinion you value? For some people, criticism is habitual, a dishonest way of making themselves look good.

What's the next step? What do I say?   The best reply comes from your head, not your heart. Having conditioned yourself to remain calm and evaluate what's been said, you'll find it easier to choose one of the following responses (or something similar):

- Postpone the issue. "I've an appointment (deadline, urgent appointment, splitting headache). Let's talk about it later." This response buys you some time.
- Be noncommittal. Members of a car pool consistently taunt their tardy member with, "You're late again." His routine reply: "So I'm told."
- Try defusing the criticism by calmly acknowledging the truth in the critic's remarks: "Maybe you're right," "That's interesting," "I never thought of it that way," all defuse the critic's ammunition and effectively terminate the discussion.

What You Ought to Know about Sexual Harassment on the Job

Shortly after being hired as an administrative assistant for a medium-sized company, a woman was approached by her supervisor for sexual favors. He kept asking her to spend time with him socially after work, repeatedly made remarks of a sexual nature to her, and suggested that her status within the company would improve if she had an affair with him. She refused; not long afterward her job was eliminated, and she was discharged. She brought suit and the company was held liable.

In another case a female worker was allegedly promised easy tasks if she consented to sexual relations with a plant foreman. Though the company lost the case, as well as a motion for a new trial, the foreman denied the charges and is still employed by the company. The cost to the corporation: $187,023 in damages.

These cases, and many others that have gotten as far as the courts, reflect a growing awareness of how serious a problem sexual harassment is being viewed. In particular, "friendly" slaps on a woman's rear, lewd jokes, and propositions, particularly those that carry a threat of reprisal if a woman refuses to submit, are no longer being viewed as acceptable forms of behavior in the workplace.

One important reason for the increased attention is the fact that the federal government and the courts now say it is illegal discrimination. The U.S. Equal Employment Opportunity Commission (EEOC) guidelines on sexual harassment, issued in November 1982, stipulate that sexual harassment is a form of illegal sex discrimination and need not be a physical act against an employee. Verbal abuse, unwelcome sexual advances, and any conduct that interferes with an employee's work performance or creates an "intimidating, hostile, or offensive working environment" may constitute sexual harassment. As long as the alleged conduct is *sexual in nature* and is *unwelcome*, a woman may have a case against her employer. Needless to say, a man harassed by a female coworker or manager has the same protection under EEOC guidelines.

In many companies, women are being encouraged to speak up if they are sexually harassed and men are discouraged from subjecting themselves to charges. For example, at General Motors, supervisors were taught in an awareness course how to refer complaints and when it's best not to interfere. The criterion: "Would you be embarrassed to see your remarks or behavior in the newspaper or described to your own family?" And American Telephone & Telegraph warns its employees that they can be fired for "repeated, offensive flirtations" or hanging "sexually suggestive" pictures. By clearly spelling out policies against sexual harassment, companies provide women with a freer atmosphere to voice their complaints.

What, then, are your options for dealing with sexual harassment?

One expert suggests that the best course is for offended employees to take rational and responsive action on their own. By doing so, a woman can channel her anger rather than holding it in and suffering from depression or the physical consequences, such as anxiety-induced pain, anorexia, and sleeplessness, which often accompany such situations.

One way suggested for handling this problem is writing a letter to the offending party. The letter should state the facts as you see them, explain how you feel and make it clear that you perceive the relationship as solely professional. A copy of the letter will also be valuable evidence if a sexual harassment charge is ultimately filed with the EEOC or appropriate state agency.

The man or woman who has been harassed might also keep a log of events. Like a letter to the offending party, this log may provide valuable evidence of repeated harassments and the steps taken to counteract them.

Talking about the problem in confidence with one or two responsible people is also helpful. Women's networks, particularly in the company, can be supportive to a woman who feels she is being victimized. If none exists, women may try to form one, letting management be aware of why they think there is a need.

Men and women might also check out their company's medical benefits to see if low-cost psychological counselling is available. Caring therapists can help the victims of sexual harassment realize that it is something that has been done *to* them; it is not anything they want or have in any way "asked for."

Organizations outside of the workplace, such as the Working Women's Institute and the Women's Legal Defense Fund are willing to lend the same kind of support and advise women of what steps to take. If no satisfactory remedy is obtained, litigation is a final step.

Mending Communication Fences

Many job problems develop around poor communication.

"Will you proofread the new employee handbook?" John's boss inquired.

"Of course."

A few weeks later the printer delivered 1,400 copies, complete with serious errors.

Why did it happen?

John assumed he'd be told when the handbook was ready to proofread. His boss assumed he'd taken care of the assignment. The manual was reprinted and rebound, an expense the company could ill afford and hadn't planned for. Because of his good employment record, John wasn't fired, but he *could* have been.

Instead of asking for specifics ("Is it ready?" "When does it go to the printer?" "If necessary, will you authorize overtime?"), John assumed he understood. Instead of clarifying his request ("It's ready for proofreading now; why not get started? It needs to be done this week; the printer is picking it up Friday."), the boss made assumptions, too.

Have you experienced job problems recently? Could faulty communications be the culprit? Broken links in the communication fence plague workers, whatever their jobs. When communications fail, production drops, mistakes occur (those that do get corrected and those that do not), sales are lost, and customers go elsewhere. The effect on productivity and profit are staggering.

So good communicators are *always* in demand.

Like fences, communication problems have two sides. As speakers we set up situations that are doomed, beginning with false assumptions. When sharing information, we assume the target audience is listening. In training new employees, we assume one explanation is enough (no questions or feedback; no demonstration or practice). Hearing problems plague many people, and others are still learning English; yet we assume our audience can hear and understand.

Sometimes we give nonverbal signals that conflict with the spoken message. Who hasn't heard someone bellow, "But I'm *not angry!*"? Generalities blur our meaning; we tell someone to do something when we mean "Do it now." or "Do it by noon today."

Some speakers use the indirect approach ("I wish someone would help me," instead of "Will you please help me?"). On the job no one has time to play guessing games. Finally, we allow sexism, bossiness, sarcasm, or rudeness to become turn-offs for the listener.

Speakers aren't the only ones at fault. An equal number of problems occur at the receiving end. We listen haphazardly—or not at all. Bombarded with information and other sounds, we tend to tune some things out. But instead of distinguishing between what's important and what's not, we sometimes tune out everything.

Another serious problem is failure to evaluate ("Is that what he meant to say?"), or ask questions ("Would you mind explaining that again?").

Want to upgrade your skills? Understanding *what the problems are* and *how to correct them* can make you a more effective communicator. Next time something you say is misunderstood, ask yourself why. Was the problem at your end? Could you have worded the statement more effectively? Like most habits, this one takes determination and practice. But perseverance pays big dividends.

Here are four coping techniques that will help you give and take orders and instructions:

1. *Accept reality.* For you, the speaker, it means *get their attention.* It may also involve providing background information. ("This is what to do, this is why we're doing it.") Timing your remarks appropriately is important and so is maintaining credibility (i.e., you come on as knowing what you're talking about).

Reality is realizing that listening requires real effort: It means focusing one's attention from something else to the speaker and the message.

2. *Be message oriented.* Unclear messages are a major cause of working mistakes. In giving instructions, clarify them by

- planning ahead (what vocabulary level will this listener understand?)
- a systematic approach ("First you press the starter.")
- providing specific information ("Do this *three* times.")
- using a positive approach
- making things as simple as you can
- using examples.

From your point of view, as a listener, the first step in message orientation is listening with a purpose. To fully participate requires a listening posture (alert, not slumped), regular feedback ("I see."), frequent eye contact and questions ("What do you mean by . . . ?").

3. *Be person centered:* Valuing others means valuing their opinion, feelings, ideas, and the like ("What do you think?"). It also helps you choose appropriate vocabulary (i.e., not "activate this positive contact," but "push this lever"). Soften harsh statements, and avoid turn-offs ("Even a monkey could do this!").

To give the speaker a chance, wait patiently and hold your fire (interruptions, criticism, and the like).

4. *Insure success.* To guarantee results, you should ask for feedback, repeat information as needed, reinforce your words with actions, and follow-up as promised to maintain your credibility.

In listening, you need to relate new information received to previous experience, take notes, ask for a demonstration and practice session (or practice on your own), and give back the instructions in your own words, "I understand that I should send these packages to all four locations to arrive by Saturday." If you begin to practice these four techniques, they'll very soon become automatic, and you will become a better than average communicator.

Coping with Change

Barb works as a finisher in a paper mill. After long days on her feet inspecting racks of paper for flaws and imperfections, she goes home worn-out. Because of the energy crisis, her union is planning to negotiate for a four-day work week. If eight hours on her feet is rough, how will she manage ten? A divorced mother of two, Barb also worries about the added cost of child care after school. Why can't things just stay the same?

Mario works for an energy conservation firm. Since they started buying computer services a few years ago, he's been the link with the supplier. Now the boss is pressuring him to take some EDP courses. When the subject comes up, Mario always promises to think about it. And he does. But he doesn't want to go back to school. Why change things?

When they face job-related changes, many other workers feel the same way. Some resist change as Barb does. Others stubbornly refuse to accept it. Those feelings are natural, but it's important to understand *why* you feel that way.

Most people feel safer and more comfortable with familiar surroundings, relationships, and procedures. Perhaps that explains why we prefer the familiar in food, clothes, and leisure activities.

But not all changes are unwelcome. Pay increases, privileged parking, and days off, since they're perceived as beneficial and risk free, win ready acceptance with most workers. Most changes, however, involve some risk. In fact, the future may be compared to a mine rich with deposits of valuable ore. Taking the ore from the ground involves the risk of accidents, cave-ins, labor problems, flooding, and more. But to leave the ore untouched because of the risks would be unthinkable. The future will bring changes. Learning to cope helps you accept change and capitalize on the opportunities it brings.

Coping with change, notes one expert, involves you in behaving, in doing, in saving, and in *acting*. When you cope successfully, you don't try to change what is causing your bad feelings. Instead you try to modify your response. Coping skills enable you to deal positively with reality and feel good about yourself.

Unfortunately, no simple formula exists. There are, however, things you can do to cope successfully when you feel threatened by change.

1. *Don't be an ostrich and bury your head.* Instead be aware of potential changes in your occupation or company. Take advantage of opportunities to be better informed about them. Attend training programs and seminars designed to acquaint you with new technology, organizational changes, and modified work roles.

2. *Be positive about change.* Review other changes that have occurred in your life, particularly those that turned out well. How did the change come about? How did you feel before it happened? What steps did you take to manage the situation? How did you feel afterwards?

3. *Accept some anxiety as natural.* Even the self-confident among us experience apprehension when change is in the offing.

4. *Be the first in your department to try something new.* Demonstrate your willingness to accept change by volunteering to be a guinea pig. Your section is being computerized, and ten people are being asked

to train for new and challenging responsibilities. Why not volunteer? Your gesture won't remove the fear, but it will enable you to prove something—to others and yourself.

5.   *Remember, you do have choices.* Suppose the worst happens, and you hate the new procedure, boss, or job role? You could be like Eraline, a housekeeper in a large nursing home. Eraline had always worked days. When a vacancy occurred on the evening shift, she was asked to fill in. The hours were terrible; she never saw her children, and she didn't feel close to her new coworkers. After three days, Eraline marched into the executive housekeeper's office and poured out her woes. Lucky she did. One week later a vacancy occurred on the day shift, and Eraline returned to her previous job. Change is risky, but in most cases it isn't irreversible.

6.   *Discuss the situation with a supervisor, role model, mentor, or counselor.* One of the best ways to cope is to discuss your feelings with someone who will listen and understand. In many cases, just talking it out will clarify the situation for you and indicate the steps you need to take.

7.   *Avoid change overload.* Too many changes, all at once, increase stress. If you're experiencing changes at work, try to postpone the move to a new apartment or going on a strict diet. Try adjusting to one change before initiating another.

8.   *If insecurity is part of the problem, reinforce your self-image.* People who believe in themselves seem to have natural coping skills.

9.   *Team up with a partner or group and face change together.* Remember when you were a teenager and you could face anything, provided you had your two best friends beside you? Granted, you're older; but knowing you have support still makes a difficult situation easier.

Reducing Fatigue on the Job

Ever come home after a tough day on the job feeling too tired to eat, too exhausted to smile, too worn out to make plans? When that happens, you feel cheated.

That worn-out feeling is no stranger to most workers. Whether you're working out of necessity and enduring a less than challenging job or throwing yourself into an exciting career, you've probably experienced it.

Really, no one in good health need be tired. Fatigue is usually brought on by boredom, worry, indecision, a sense of inferiority, and little nagging fears. If your job is a constant source of excitement and stimulation, you may not experience end-of-the-day fatigue. However, most jobs aren't *that* exciting. The suggestions that follow will help you alleviate fatigue.

1. *Reduce sources of job stress.* What aspects of your job drive you up the wall? Once you answer that question, you're on your way to dealing with them.

Among the causes of stress identified by Jude West of the University of Iowa's Center for Labor and Management are: role ambiguity (not knowing what you're supposed to do), role conflict (personal problems that conflict with the job), role overload or underload (too much or too little work), changing work shifts, tight deadlines, and unfair treatment in pay or job status. Once you've figured out what exactly is bothering you, you'll be able to cope with the problem better.

2. *Give yourself more change of pace.* Most work schedules are set up around morning and afternoon coffee breaks and, of course, lunch. Breaks during which you drink the same thing at the same place with the same people having the same conversation day after day become a tiresome routine. Instead, try escaping psychologically once in a while with simple meditation or a stimulating discussion group. Or escape physically with a brisk walk or quiet moments under a tree.

3. *Give yourself more to look forward to after work.* Which after-work activities give you a psychological lift? Sinking into a comfortable chair with a favorite book and soft music may be your ideal, but is it *enough*? You might want to try cultivating an artistic hobby, such as painting or crafts; active sports, such as jogging or tennis; or getting together with family or friends. If you have family responsibilities, you can't do them all, but try at least one.

4. *Reduce sources of on-the-job fatigue.* One way to do this is to assess your capability levels and schedule your work accordingly. If you work best in the morning, try to get the most important things done early in the day. Another technique has to do with organizing your work space more efficiently. If you're in an office, ask yourself how your desk, phone, files, and the like could be arranged for greater convenience.

5. *Take better care of yourself.* If you're suffering from work-related fatigue, the problem could be that you're not eating right. Eating balanced meals and healthy food has worked wonders for many work-weary Americans. Try eating "junk food" for one week, and record or tape something about how tired you are at the same hour every evening. During the second week, eat healthy, balanced meals every day and record your feelings again. It goes without saying that exercise, regular sleep, and moderation should be a part of your self-help program.

6. *Discover that "passive" is boring; action is a turn-on.* If you've ever exhausted yourself watching Saturday afternoon football, you've already discovered that inertia is a source of fatigue. Try to get some type of physical exercise at least three times a week. It could be anything from a noontime exercise class at the local "Y" to after-work bowling with the company team.

7. *Find more to like about your job.* The best job is one that offers you a continuing challenge. You'll like your job better if it demands your best, doing useful important work, and the opportunity to participate in work-related decisions. If any or all of these factors are missing, try discussing the matter with your supervisor.

8. *Put more "people power" into your life.* Ever notice that some people give you a lift while others drag you down? Try spending more time with the former, less with the latter. Look for those who can invigorate you.

As the day-to-day pressures of living increase, the ability to cope becomes an essential skill. Learning to prevent fatigue offers you a bonus. Banish fatigue, and you'll enjoy a fuller, richer life.

Nonsmokers' Rights

Sarah G. and Jennifer P. worked side-by-side in the secretarial pool of a large company. Sarah smoked two packs of cigarettes a day. Jennifer was a nonsmoker. One day Jennifer complained to her supervisor about the physical discomfort the cigarette smoke was causing her, explaining that she wanted advice on the most tactful solution to the problem. Her supervisor, sympathetic to Jennifer's situation, moved her to another area of the office.

More and more, nonsmoking employees are speaking-up for their "rights" to work in a healthy environment; and employers are responding.

According to a recent survey by the National Interagency Council on Smoking and Health, 15 percent of U.S. business concerns have antismoking programs and one-third are interested in developing or expanding existing programs.

A vanguard case in the issue of nonsmokers' rights in the workplace was *Shimp vs. New Jersey Bell Telephone Co.* Donna Shimp, who was severely allergic to cigarette smoke, claimed that her employer, New Jersey Bell Telephone Co., caused her to work in an unsafe environment by refusing to ban smoking in her office. She brought suit in 1976. The judge's ruling in the Shimp case made it clear that cigarette smoke would be considered a health hazard.

Although the Tobacco Institute would disagree with such a finding, there is quantitative, new evidence indicating that nonsmokers are harmed by the passive intake of cigarette smoke. Long-term exposure to tobacco smoke causes respiratory impairment to nonsmokers. Research data has shown that nonsmokers regularly exposed to smoke have "test scores" similar to those who smoked up to eleven cigarettes a day.

What, then, can you do if you are a nonsmoker and your company is not living up to its obligation to provide a safe and healthy working environment?

Begin by looking at what other companies are doing. IBM, for example, has issued guidelines to managers to accommodate nonsmoking employees. The corporation has "no-smoking" signs available to its staff, and classrooms and meeting rooms are divided into smoking and nonsmoking sections. One such company, Cybertek Computer Products, Inc., in Los Angeles, offered its 140 U.S. employees $500 a year to stop smoking. Blue Cross/Blue Shield of New Jersey has on-the-job smoking clinics for interested companies.

You might ask management to institute similar programs. But before doing so, familiarize yourself with the various organizations concerned with the issue. Your local chapter of the American Lung Association or American Cancer Society is likely to have information that would be helpful. The New York City Division of the American Cancer Society (19 W. 56 St., New York, N.Y., 10019), for instance, has available, a booklet entitled, "Nonsmokers' Rights," prepared by the committee on Consumer Affairs, New York County Lawyers' Association. The booklet is not restricted to nonsmokers' rights in the workplace, although it does include a listing entitled "factories." Another booklet, devoted exclusively to nonsmokers' rights in the workplace, is "Smoke-free Work Areas," published by Environmental Improvement Associates, 111 Chestnut Street, Salem, N.J., 08079.

The Group Against Smokers' Pollution (GASP), an active antismoking group, will send you, for 50¢, "The Non-Smokers Liberation Guide. A Manual of Revolutionary Tactics and Strategies to Save the Breathing Rights of Non-Smokers Everywhere." They also have posters, signs, and buttons available for a company-sponsored campaign. Write GASP, P.O. Box 632, College Park, MD 20740. A pamphlet entitled "Non-Smoking Employees Guide to Preservation of Unemployment Insurance Benefits" is available, free of charge, from GASP Legal Fund, P.O. Box 1061, Berkeley, CA 94701.

Once you have an idea of how the various organizations have been successful in promulgating nonsmokers' rights at work, you'll have ammunition with which to approach management. William Alli, cofounder of Federal Employees for Nonsmokers' Rights, however, points out that situations vary from office to office and often depend on an individual's willingness to be assertive. While he advocates operating through a union organization where one exists, he cautions against joining a union with the specific intention of working on the health and safety committees.

He also pointed out that fostering *awareness* of the health hazards of cigarette smoke aids your effectiveness in instituting a program that would, at the very least, restrict smoking in the workplace.

Litigation is, of course, a last resort, other efforts having been made to establish your rights. Smokers have rights, too, smokers will argue. However, as Judge Gruccio stated in the Shimp case, "The right of an individual to risk his or her own health does not include the right to jeopardize the health of those who must remain around him or her in order to properly perform the duties of their jobs."

He further pointed out: "The company, New Jersey Bell Telephone, already has in effect a rule that cigarettes are not to be smoked around telephone equipment. The rationale behind the rule is that the machines are extremely sensitive and can be damaged by the smoke. Human beings are also very sensitive and can be damaged by smoke. . . . A company that has demonstrated such concern for its mechanical components should have at least as much concern for its human beings."

Stress: the "Hurry Sickness"

You're about to ask for a job. Or a raise. Or your performance review is coming up. Or you're meeting the new boss.

Your palms sweat. Your heart pounds. Your mouth is dry. Maybe you're having trouble breathing. Often you're frightened or angry, tense and upset.

You're experiencing a classic case of stress on the job. Stress is the body's reaction to danger, fear, or anger. And it doesn't make any difference whether the cause is real or imagined. In today's fast-paced working world of fast change, complexity, and new work styles, it's hard to make the adjustments needed to stay on an even keel. It's no wonder that many have named stress the "hurry sickness."

In the "hurry sickness," when the brain begins to scramble signals to the body, or when the signals become too frequent, or pressures and deadlines crowd you, the tension that arises often causes physical symptoms.

Stress, though, is not just an isolated reaction to a problem or a nasty situation. It builds up from a progression of everyday setbacks that can affect your job performance, family life—even life itself. If you've ever had a backache, or a pain in your neck, lost your appetite, noticed an increase in your smoking or drinking patterns, have been beset by strange anxieties, insomnia, or depression, you've also experienced these stress symptoms. When these symptoms become constant, they can bring on serious illness.

People who experience it most are often like Harry, the workaholic whose day never ends. He comes in early, leaves late, and takes work home; and he never objects. It's Molly, the gem of a secretary, who worries all night if she has left one single task undone; and she frequently works late. It's Joanna, the fireball waitress, who runs a marathon on-the-double through the lunch hour, then cleans up the tables and counters and replenishes her service station. It's Mike, the accountant, who double and triple checks his work, often until the wee hours of the night, because he doesn't trust himself not to make an error.

It's interesting to note that it usually isn't the boss who gets hit with stress syndrome. It's his staff. As people move up the management ladder, they tend to get healthier!

What causes stress for you on the job? Unrealistic career goals, fellow workers, a too-burdensome work load, information overload, boredom, your position in the company, the lack of job security, too rapid or too slow promotion, or possibly even success.

Job stress is one of the commonest causes of lost work time. Stress-related disease and accidents have become so frequent, in fact, that more than fifteen states have approved benefits in cases of disability stemming from job stress. How can you avoid or at least deal with it?

There are ways to manage stress. Immediate problems may range from buying earplugs to shut out assembly-line noise to deciding to seek psychiatric help.

First it is of prime importance to keep your body in shape to better weather stressful times:

- *Exercise regularly.* Jog, if you're up to it, but exercise enough to achieve relaxation.
- *Eat well.* Practice good nutrition—balanced meals (no skipped meals or ten-minute lunches). Cut down your intake of caffeine, nicotine, and sugar. Caffeine is a sure stress maker.
- *Learn some relaxing techniques.* Yoga, meditation, or other deep, relaxing regimens. Classes in one or more of these techniques are available locally. See your yellow pages.

Now you're ready for some changes in the way you handle your everyday life. Here are some steps you can take to cut down stressful living, make your working day more pleasant, and perhaps even prolong your life:

- Don't waste time with people who don't return your friendship. Remember, everyone doesn't have to be your friend.
- Take pleasure in simple things: a walk, a game with your kids, a good book, a garden, or a hobby.
- Concentrate on the pleasurable moments of the day. There are always bright spots. Seek them out.
- Re-establish your self-confidence after setbacks by dwelling on the many successes you've had.
- Don't put off unpleasant tasks; tackle them and save yourself the nagging stress of unfinished work.

- Realize everyone doesn't have the capacity or the temperament to be president, or even manager, of your department. Set realistic work goals.
- Love yourself enough to make the world pleasant and productive for those around you.

These days, faced with recession, layoffs, and high interest rates, most people suffer from more stress than ever before. If you have stress problems, you're not crazy, and you're certainly not alone. Simply acknowledging these two facts may be the first step in coping. Incorporating the approaches listed above into your life style may take the sting out of the stressful situations that are bound to happen.

Coping with Manipulation

Bosses and coworkers who openly manipulate others shouldn't expect to have a lot of friends. At least that's the opinion most people hold. Increasingly the term *manipulator* is used to describe underhanded, power-grabbing tactics. No wonder the word makes us wary, suspicious, even fearful.

But surprisingly, the word's real meaning is neither positive or negative, as people studying this subject point out. It's a term that means a person who takes things in hand. Whether manipulation is positive or negative, then, depends on the motivations and intentions of the person who does it.

Since it's often associated with destructive behavior, the concept of manipulation can be confusing. When is it a plus; when is it a minus; and how do you tell the difference? It's a minus in a situation where employees have their titles changed, job descriptions rewritten, and salaries increased, only to find they are doing the same work as before, according to management consultant Marion S. Kellogg. Still another example would be the small retailer who holds on to student employees long after they're ready for the next level of career advancement.

When manipulation represents a bid for power, you'll recognize the clues—the motives are selfish; the methods, devious; the planning, secretive. The element of secrecy also explains why the person being manipulated feels "ganged up" on.

Positive manipulation, on the other hand, is characterized by openness and honesty. Though inexperienced, Cara is her boss's choice for the new bookkeeping position. He's urging her to sign up for a couple of bookkeeping courses at the community college as a way of growing professionally and increasing her career options. But since he doesn't control the promotion decision, he doesn't want to dangle an enticement he may later be unable to produce.

52

Another characteristic is balance in terms of effort and rewards, distribution of work, and the like. Positive manipulation reinforces good work and encourages people to be more productive and innovative.

Typically, manipulation occurs in three arenas of career life. The first involves environment. Typical of the way we change environment to meet our needs is the individual who, upon moving into a new office, must rearrange the furniture, add plants and accessories, even request new draperies. In less than a year with the firm, Sally has used her poor eyesight to capture the only office with an outside window. Frank finds building a special relationship with the shared secretary results in preferential treatment for his work.

Another typical setting is the small group, in which leadership is the prize. The manipulator may have a conscious intention to exploit leadership for his or her own ends. But unfortunately for such a person, the leadership may not be accepted; his or her authority is questioned and orders are not followed.

The third arena is management. You might say that manipulation is inherent in it, that is, if one regards manipulation as getting other people to do what one wants them to do. Sometimes management allows participation at a superficial level to give employees a feeling of involvement. If, in fact, all decisions are being made by management, employees *feel* manipulated.

When you feel yourself being manipulated, you may be tempted to give in. Don't.

1. *When the situation is suspect*, examine it closely. Is this manipulation? Has it more negative or more positive aspects? If you're still uncertain, an examination of the situation at least warns you to move with caution.

2. *Acknowledge to yourself what's going on*. When you suspect manipulation, don't sweep it under the carpet. If it makes you fearful, remember that even in its negative form manipulation doesn't spell disaster.

3. *Respond assertively*. Try using sentences that describe your feelings ("I'm not comfortable about what's going on."). Say *no* firmly; people will respect you for it. Try a workable compromise to arrive at a more satisfactory solution.

4. *Consider your options*. Can you remove yourself from the manipulator's sphere? Insulate yourself against power-grabbing tactics? Ask for a transfer or make a job change? Changing your environment won't free you of all manipulation forever, but you might find yourself in a less manipulative situation.

5. *If circumstances force you into manipulative behavior, choose the positive form.*

Working for a Woman: Some New Data

Sam, a career-minded, junior supervisor for a large manufacturing firm, had been told he was being transferred to another department to work for the new purchasing director. The move seemed like a promotion, and Sam was excited about the change. But when he met his new boss, he was crestfallen; the new boss was a woman. As far as Sam was concerned, working for a woman meant a demotion in status in the company.

Rather than attempt to find out what his boss and the job were like, Sam decided to request a transfer or find a new job. He probably would have been better off staying where he was. This particular manager had a history of working closely with capable junior people—male and female—and training them for promotion to executive positions.

Sam's reaction illustrates the problems associated with a relatively new phenomenon: the female boss. As more women receive advance degrees and enter the work force, they inevitably are moving into management positions in significant numbers. In fact, according to the U.S. Department of Labor, the number of women managers has more than doubled since 1969. But no matter how capable a boss a woman may be, many employees of both sexes are resistant to working for one. You have probably heard other employees say, "I've worked for a woman, but I'll never do it again." However, the likelihood that you *will* work for one at some point in your career is constantly increasing.

Men will probably have a harder time adjusting to working with women bosses than will women, seeing the situation as a threat to their own stature and masculinity. Others will not be able to throw off the conditioning that men and women have social relationships but not working ones.

However, working for women can have some distinct advantages, whether you are a man or a woman. Many people have found female bosses much more valuable in furthering their training and job advancement than men. Two recent studies illustrate this.

A recent study of sixty-eight male and one hundred and two female managers at work showed that female managers were found to be twice as accessible to their employees as their male counterparts (which, of course, means that male managers were half as accessible as the women). More women than men actually encouraged their staffs to seek them out, and many women (but no men) habitually left their offices to see whether subordinates needed them or to inquire whether things were going well. Even accessible male managers were less likely to seek out their employees than to say, "If they need me, they know where to find me."

Interestingly none of the women in the study said they were usually unreachable, while some men said they maintain a barrier so that they could work without being interrupted. And quite a few men who saw themselves as accessible were perceived as not being so by their employees, while no women fell into that category. This research suggests that on your own job you are likely to get more direct contact, help, and communication from female executives.

The second survey, conducted by an executive-search firm, questioned successful women executives about mentors, that is, more experienced people in the company who provide career help and support to less experienced workers. Since women have only been in high-level positions for a relatively short time, it is not surprising that 85 percent of the women executives did *not* have a woman mentor as an aid to rising on the job. However, 80 percent of the women said they now serve as a mentor for lower-level women. Furthermore, about three-quarters of those surveyed feel the mentor system is still important to women who wish to achieve success in their careers.

For women, a female boss presents a perfect opportunity for a mentor. If you have a female boss or expect to work for one and are apprehensive about the situation, it is well worth giving it a chance. Data, such as those provided by the studies mentioned here, indicate that women are far more willing to act as mentors to help you adjust and improve at work and to pay more attention to your career development. How should you handle it? Approach the situation with enthusiasm and show that you are willing to work with others. Regardless of gender these are the characteristics necessary to succeed in your career and to attract a mentor (especially if she's your boss); so just apply them to this new situation.

No matter what your work situation, knowing that your boss is concerned about you and your work can vastly improve your working environment and, in turn, make you a more productive employee. Being more productive obviously increases your chances for promotion.

Several experts caution, however, about taking advantage of your woman boss's accessibility. Be careful not to become too dependent on her willingness to help. Try to solve problems on your own before asking your boss to solve them for you. And avoid bringing personal problems to your boss if at all possible. She may be willing to help, but a maternal or sisterly relationship with her can rarely be beneficial. Treat her like a professional and chances are she'll treat you the same way.

MOVING AHEAD

You're only telling half the truth when you say, "I want a job." At any time and in any economy, there are many jobs that go vacant simply because people don't want to do them. Why? Because they're boring, menial, dangerous, or require heavy labor. They're not the jobs you want. What you really want (so, admit it) is a *good* job. Even when you're warned how severe the competition is for the upscale jobs, the interesting ones that earn you high status, a good salary, and entertaining projects, you go on trying for the plums. After all, even if your chances are only one in twenty, there *is* that possibility that you'll be the lucky one. So you keep on trying. Somehow, you think, things will work out. You'll make them work out.

A highly motivated attitude, persistence, and determination are half the battle toward winning the hotly competed-for managerial or professional slots in solid, profitable companies—the jobs you want. But you need an extra edge over the competition: an awareness of the market in which you're competing. How do you get your work act together and do so faster than the rest of the pack? For a start, prepare yourself to handle new responsibilities, and even new kinds of jobs. Don't just react to on-the-job situations; anticipate them. It'll be noticed.

Don't stop there. Plan your work time and career with the same care that you planned your education and job-hunt. Take a look at your basic skills. Is there any way you can upgrade them or add new ones? Explore new tools like the home computer. Demonstrate your flexibility by adapting to a change in your job description or work environment, and learn to let your management see how well you function.

After all, if you can do all this, you're *someone*. Not a faceless, expendable social security number, not a cog in the corporate wheel, but a valuable person who deserves to be rewarded.

4

The Decade as a Marker of Career Expectations

Managers in their thirties are still willing to take risks and move on to new jobs, but their approach may be more cautious and marked by a reevaluation of goals. Executives in their forties start to get restless; if they don't make career changes now, they'll have fewer opportunities to do so later on. The fifties are marked by feelings of panic or distress over being pushed out of a job before retirement. Companies are less reluctant to let go a fifty-year-old executive than one who's in his or her sixties and nearing retirement.

Here are some helpful suggestions, a sort of "survival kit" for managers.

- When your job has become routine and no longer challenges you, that's the time to start looking around discreetly.
- It's just as easy—and a whole lot more profitable—to work for a good salary as it is to work for peanuts. In general, don't make a job switch unless a raise goes with it.
- Never mind what havoc job-hoppers wreak in the companies they abandon; the man or woman who job-hops rapidly becomes unpopular. Too many employers in too short a time may make people wonder what's wrong with you.
- These days you can't afford to drift. Take stock of your career regularly. Do you even have a career plan? If so, are you on course? If you're not, consider the alternatives to changing companies, such

as changing jobs within your company or transfering to another department.

Above all make sure you fit the qualifications of a job. Don't promise more than you can deliver. These are two prime danger areas for managers and nonmanagers alike. Remember, moving up in the business world demands two things: strong goal orientation and no lack of self-confidence.

Getting and keeping management positions call for demonstrating that you are motivated to do the job and to make solid contributions to the company's goals; and demonstrating the ability to continue personal growth and flexibility to meet new challenges. Most of all, be prepared to work hard and conscientiously.

Even more valuable, especially to those starting out in management or considering it as a new field to look into, is getting a better education when the opportunity presents itself. There is no such thing as too much investigating or preparing for a new job before one accepts it.

Even during a period of high unemployment, in our world of ever-changing technologies there's a persistent need for bright, innovative people. But if you don't thrive on responsibility and risk-taking, you might consider avoiding careers in which you'll be required to manage others or change your job regularly.

Training: Vital for Career Survival

You see the headlines, read the articles, and view the fantastic new machinery on TV, and you know that the whole working world is in the process of changing right under your feet. The robots aren't coming to the factory floor; they're already here. The office of the future is becoming the *now* office—one with new machinery and new ways of working already available. They're about to install a new computer in your company or perhaps individual desk computers or terminals. How is all this going to affect you?

Awareness of imminent or actual change underlies many of the problems companies are experiencing. One factor in the widely publicized air controllers strike was the concern for job security at a time when new technical advances may replace many of these specialists. Unions, it is being reported, are now much more involved in negotiating job security for members than increasing their income. Meanwhile, plant workers in the South and white-collar workers everywhere, including low-level programmers, are beginning to listen to the overtures of organized labor—mostly because of fear that their jobs may disappear.

What can you do about it? Is there an answer to this ongoing "career" shock?

Yes. In one word: training.

While today's jobs may be threatened by the changing workplace, whole new categories of jobs are being created with new demands for personnel. Many companies are meeting these new staffing problems with current personnel but retrained. The American Society for Training and Development conservatively estimates that industry is spending at least $30 billion a year in employee training, and the cost is probably a lot more.

Today, when people are laid off, they are not forgotten. Many companies start retraining them for new and needed jobs. A recent *Wall Street Journal* story was headlined, "As Ranks of Skilled Jobless Grow, Efforts to Retrain Them for New Careers Begin." It quotes a Labor Department official as saying, "These displaced workers are an asset. . . . The big problem ahead of us is going to be to fit them to the new jobs out there."

The purpose of training is to increase your worth as an employee. Trained workers are more productive, which is the key to profits for the company. As a corollary, as you become a more valuable worker, geared to operating successfully in the new work environment, you gain a better measure of job security.

The moral: Get into training *now* to prepare yourself for the new jobs and new careers to come. Even if you don't have access to training through your company, you can retrain yourself. Two case histories demonstrate the real value training may have for you.

Hank got his training at a $16 million company training center that features the use of color films, video tapes, "user friendly" computer programs, and simulators that reproduce closely what actually happens on the job (simulators once limited to aircraft pilot training). He learned a critically needed skill in the petroleum field where his company is a leading service firm. Because of a proliferation of drilling rigs and the existing need for workers to man and service them, the training packed what might ordinarily require two to three years into an intensive six-month course. Courses were crowded: fifty-five people jammed into a lab designed for twenty-five, for example. It takes forty to sixty well-trained crew members to make an oil-drilling rig functional; and in many cases they all come from outside the oil industry through training.

Hank's reward for the long hours and tough courses? A high-paying job in the dynamic energy industry and a background of skills and knowledge that will be valuable for a long time to come.

Sara began her job in the local jewelry store like anyone else: waiting on customers, showing watches and rings and other items. Though a prestige store, it is a relatively small business and has no formal training programs for its people. Sara, however, began reading the trade publications in the field, the retail jewelry manuals used in the business, and expanded this to outside reading and study.

Before long she could identify various stones, talk about them to customers knowledgeably and with enthusiasm. The store owners, noting her growing competence, introduced her to the sophisticated equipment used to examine and evaluate diamonds and other gems, and worked with her to help her understand the business side of selling. She now is able to deal with some of the firm's most affluent customers and discuss investment-quality gems and custom-designed settings. Business courses at night and industry seminars on marketing skills are broadening her capabilities. Sara is in line to manage a new branch her company is opening in a posh suburb. Her on-the-job self-training has paid off.

How and where you get your training will vary according to your own job, your employer, what you want to be, and where you want to go. But for the 80's, "training" is the magic word to help you over the hurdles as the revolution in the workplace broadens.

How do you find out what skills are going to be needed and what kind of training will prepare you? One useful source is the Department of Labor's *Occupational Outlook Quarterly*, which provides just that type of information. Another source may be the personnel department of your company. There's also a substantial volume of information appearing in career-oriented books (see Bibliography). Also check the local community colleges, the adult education courses in your area, and, of course, the employment pages of your newspaper.

Continuing Education: The New Wave of Learning

Right now, about one out of three adult Americans is involved in the fast-growing phenomenon called "continuing education." That term is being used to describe any training you may take after completing high school or college. And it refers to programs ranging from formal classroom courses provided by local school boards and community colleges (at costs ranging from free to $200 per course), to mail order correspondence courses ($100 to $1,000 or more), and even to inexpensive, self-paced instruction texts ($20 to $100).

If you're not already part of this new wave of learning, is it something you should be considering? Definitely! It's not only one of the ways in which to keep up with accelerating changes in our whole environment (you might find a course in tax-return preparation or automobile maintenance a practical way to help combat inflation, for example), but it is likely to be helpful to you in career terms as well. Additionally, you may be able to obtain college credits for your continuing education efforts.

The decade of the 80's will see the rewards going to the knowledgeable—those who bring skills and sophisticated know-how to meet the needs of our demanding technology.

Many of the courses available are intended to help you sharpen your current job skills. As a secretary, for example, you may want to learn to operate a word processor or acquire another language to broaden your job horizons. If you're doing janitorial or maintenance work, you may study for a stationary engineer's license to be able to operate energy-efficient building heating systems. Programmers take extra courses to learn new computer systems or programming languages. Journalists take photography courses to add another dimension to their reporting. In fact, there's almost no subject that someone isn't studying somewhere in the U.S. at the moment you're reading this.

Often, when the courses are work related, they are paid for by employers, who see this as a way of "growing their own" experts in various skills or fields and who recognize also that such study leads to more efficiency, higher motivation, and greater job satisfaction.

Though no job is totally "recession proof," the more skills and background you have, the more likely you are to be retained when times are hard. You'll be more flexible, more capable in handling varied assignments than your fellow worker who lacks this extra background. And, of course, continuing education will help you qualify for more openings if you *do* have to job-hunt, as well as demonstrate to a potential employer your initiative, worth, and versatility.

What if the continuing education courses you want aren't available locally?

One alternative is to begin a good reading program, to pick up as much information as you can about the area in which you're interested. Of course, there are some skills you can't learn from books alone: carpentry, for example. Then, too, most people have problems maintaining a study program on their own. However, for subjects like bookkeeping or math skills, there are so-called "self-paced instruction books" or "programmed learning texts" whose question-and-answer formats help you both understand the material and test yourself to see that you are indeed learning.

Another approach is correspondence courses. These generally provide one "class" at a time, including a test, which you complete and mail back. Your corrected test is returned along with the next "class." Some courses require expensive equipment, usually supplied as part of the course fee. The equipment can range from a computer terminal to a kit of tools. Such "extras," of course, add to the cost.

The new "hot line" system, which allows you, as a home-study student, to call toll-free with your questions regarding study materials, is increasingly popular and adds to the effectiveness of such training.

How do you choose continuing education courses? The best way is to talk to others who've already taken them. You may also get guidance from the various groups and trade associations who accredit such studies. Here are some of the major ones:

For college-level training, including two-year associate degree programs for technicians and similar careers, consult the quarterly directory of the American Council of Education, One DuPont Circle, Washington, DC, 20036. Many full-time colleges and junior colleges will accept home-study courses for degree credit if the ACE has accredited them.

Most good home-study programs are produced by organizations affiliated with the National Home Study Council, 1601 18th Street, NW, Washington, DC, 20009. Write to them for a list of accredited organizations.

Another trade association, the Council for Noncollegiate Continuing Education, also offers a list. Their address is 530 East Main Street, Richmond, VA, 23219.

Get Ahead by Managing Your Time

We all know about workaholics—people who are compulsive workers and carry the job with them all the time. But some of us only *look* like workaholics. We work harder and longer and get less done than we should because we haven't learned some of the basics of managing our time on the job. The better you perform in today's shaky economy, the better chance you have not only of keeping your job but of making that important move up. Many consultants feel that an ability to operate efficiently within the forty to fifty hours a week you spend at work is a prime factor in making progress on the job.

Here, then, is a group of key recommendations on time management culled from a number of different sources, together with some recommended reading to give you further insights into handling your working time to best advantage.

1. Find out how you *really* spend your time on the job. When the day goes by so fast you hardly notice it, but you still haven't gotten important tasks accomplished, it's valuable to know why. One often recommended technique is to set up a daily log and keep notes every fifteen minutes of how your workday is being spent. It is tough to do this, particularly when you're under a lot of pressure; but the payoff is worthwhile because, once you have the actual data, you can begin to see where your time goes (responding to telephone calls, being involved in meetings, talking with your boss, and so on). You can then act to eliminate, or at least minimize, the unnecessary activities that cut into your working time. The secret to good time management is to substitute consciously selected activities for those that are more-or-less forced on you. In order to do this, you must act on step two: determining goals.

2. Many people work for years without really understanding their working function or why their job exists. If you are going to manage your time effectively, you need to take a look not only at *what* you're doing on the job but its basic purpose and value to the organization. In many companies, work is so fragmented that this may be hard to find out. You may work on figures that come in from various branches, and your work may then be included with much other information that is fed into a computer, for example. Once you know what the figures are used for and what they tell about the organization, you can focus on the importance of the various aspects of your work and get an insight into what your working goals should be. This, in turn, leads to point three: priorities.

3. Now that you have a firm grasp of what you should be accomplishing, you can determine the relative priorities of your work load. A very effective working technique is to set your priorities each day, making a list of both the short-term and the long-term projects you should be working on. Then, apply the ABC Priority System made famous by consultant Alan Lakein. Beside each item on your list place an A for high priority, B for medium priority, and C for low priority. You can break each of these down further into A-1, A-2, A-3, and so on, providing a clear structure on which to build your workday. With this system, figure that A projects are those to be done the same day and B if you have time. You may find that C items never get done at all. Your list will change daily as new projects or work assignments occur.

4. How about those long-term, important projects? For many people, these are often the most difficult to manage: the big report the boss is going to need next month or the inventory that should be finished this quarter. Too often these get postponed until the last minute and become crises. How can you manage them? An old American Indian proverb goes, "The way to cross a lake is to cross the lake." In other words, don't put off doing what has to be done. Get at it! It is tempting to postpone the big job "until I get all the regular work out of the way," or "until things aren't so hectic." Instead, try these steps:

- Sit down and write out what has to be done on the project, dividing these tasks into individual steps—the smallest steps possible. This list gives you a blueprint from which to work.
- Schedule a step or two each day and give these an A priority. If possible, set a regular block of time aside specifically for this project.
- Try to deal with the most difficult or time-consuming steps early in order to relieve the pressures on you.
- Keep tabs on your progress by checking off on your written description those jobs or steps you've completed.
- Have deadlines for the big sections of the project to help keep you on schedule.
- Review as you go, to keep your perspective on the overall project clear and fresh.

These four points really are just the tip of the iceberg in terms of the subject of managing your time on the job (and off). Fortunately, there are a number of useful books on the subject that can give you more detailed ideas and insights for working smarter rather than harder by making the most of your time on the job. See the list of sources at the back of this book.

Choosing a Role Model

The man Hank admires most is his boss, Tony, who worked his way up and now owns his own business selling and servicing air conditioners. Tony has a real way with people; all the customers like him, and Hank wants to become successful, like Tony.

When Nancy started to work for the insurance company, she immediately established a relationship with Helen, a division vice-president. From Helen, Nancy hopes to learn what it takes to move up in the company.

If you've been tuned in to "career talk," chances are you've heard a lot about role models, mentors, sponsors, and patrons. Such people can play an important role in your career.

What the role model and mentor have in common is their ability to help others grow. Hank's admiration for Tony makes him try harder. He wants to please Tony; he also wants to follow the older man's example and some day own *his* own business. Nancy deliberately chose a mentor, someone who could help further her career. Helen is flattered by the younger woman's attention and glad to help a talented young person achieve her career goals.

Some people, of course, don't choose a mentor. Instead, they are recognized as having unrealized potential. Some successful people enjoy choosing an individual and sponsoring that person's climb up the career ladder.

From a role model, you can learn a great deal about the personal and professional style appropriate to your profession. Watching an experienced colleague, you learn how to act in delicate situations. Together, you chart a course through the troubled waters of company strategy and politics.

As you look more closely at the mentor–protégé relationship, you may wish you had some guidelines. Hopefully, the suggestions that follow will help you make the right decisions.

1. Try to earn the confidence and respect of superiors; your chances of aligning yourself with a suitable sponsor will be enhanced. After an outstanding performance, some people tend to slack off. Winning the confidence of superiors demands consistency in behavior and performance.

2. Choose someone with a positive attitude. Associate with people who are "positive thinkers and optimistic." Someone with a positive outlook is more apt to take a positive view of your ability and potential.

3. Don't wait to be chosen. Worship from afar can be inspiring; you may even learn from the one you admire. However, successful role-modeling usually demands a closer, more open relationship. If you are hesitant about making the first move, why not ask for advice? Helping you advance your career could be as rewarding for the mentor as for you.

4. Pick someone in the same company, advises a New York job-counselling specialist. "Seek out someone in power (who may or may not be your boss and may even be in a totally different department), but someone you'd like to emulate and learn from; and find out if that person is willing to help sponsor you."

5. Don't limit your choice to someone of the same sex. Opposite-sex mentors can be extremely helpful. Many women have moved up in the organization because a successful male boss recognized their potential for management.

6. Allow the relationship to grow and develop. Worthwhile relationships don't happen overnight. You will have to earn the trust and confidence of your mentor, and, as is the case with all relationships, that takes time.

7. Choose someone whose style and values you share at least to some degree. Suppose the individual you admire is aggressively ambitious, not the way you operate. Most people find it impossible to be comfortable with a style that is wrong for them. Though you may have much to learn from the aggressively ambitious person, you may have to draw the line at adopting his or her style.

8. Look for qualities of maturity, leadership, and philosophy, rather than just success. Some individuals succeed through singleness of purpose and willingness to make sacrifices. You might not be willing to make the same sacrifices. Success alone doesn't qualify one to be a role model.

9. Choose someone who is willing to help you grow—one you can learn from. And most important, do not be intimidated by others who happen to be smarter. Growth, after all, encompasses making the most of opportunities, savoring the experience as well as the result, giving as well as receiving, and fulfilling one's individual potential.

Good Business Writing—a Key to Getting Ahead

Do you panic at the thought of having to write a memo? Is writing a business letter the worst part of your job? Does the idea of having to prepare a written report upset you for days in advance? Join the crowd.

Business writing for most of us is a major chore. Yet business literally thrives on "paperwork," and if you're going to get ahead you have to develop the ability to prepare business communications in minimum time and with maximum readability and clarity.

Fortunately, such writing isn't an art—it's a skill, a set of habits that can be acquired by knowing and practicing just three basic steps.

Step One: Think first.   Ask yourself, "What is the one main point I want to get across?" Try to sum it up in a single sentence and write that sentence down. Why is this point important to you? Is it important to your reader? Should it be? Why? (What's in it for him?)

To answer this question, you need to know your reader. If you know him or her personally, try to imagine this person sitting across the desk from you as you write so that you're talking together. If not, find out something about the person you're addressing before you write so that you can "imagine" an audience for your message.

Another important question in thinking about your reader is, "What do I want the reader of my letter or memo to do as the result of receiving it?" Unless your written message motivates him or her to take action—the right action—it's a failure.

Step Two: Do a rough draft.   You begin the actual writing. If you have devoted some time and energy to stage one, this should be the quickest and easiest phase of all. You have your reader clearly in mind. You know what you want to say to him or her. Now say it. Follow the advice of a famous expert on clear writing and "talk on paper."

Many people find this difficult to do because they are paralyzed by fear of failure. Instead of having an imaginary audience that they're talking to, they have an imaginary English teacher in the same room looking over their shoulders. They think they have to have a perfect outline. They worry about spelling and grammar. They remember "rules" from the classroom, such as, "Never say I," "Don't begin a sentence with but or and," or "Never end a sentence with a preposition." If that's your situation, you should know that such "rules" are mere opinions and outmoded ones at that. They're the enemies of simple, natural writing—the kind that people like to read.

Forget rules. Write quickly and even carelessly. Mistakes can be corrected later. Write it just as it comes into your mind, and don't let the flow of your thoughts be dammed up by the critic inside your brain. His day will come soon enough.

Now, put your rough draft aside. (You may, at this stage, want to have it rough-typed double-spaced so that it will be easier to make corrections.) Try to allow yourself enough time, between rough draft and revision, so that you can come to it with a fresh outlook.

Step Three: Revise.   This revision stage is the most important. Regrettably, it's also the one that most business writers skip. The reason, no doubt, is to save time. But hard-to-understand, ineffective reports waste time and money for the sender and the receiver as well. If it's only going to end up in the circular file, why bother to send it at all? The real hard work of writing comes with rewriting. Now is the time to let your "critic" loose on your work.

Ask yourself the following questions about your rough draft:

"Does my opening paragraph contain anything that would make my reader want to read on?" In holding your reader's interest, "you" is the most powerful word you can use.

"Do I state my main point clearly, preferably near the beginning?" The sooner your reader knows what your message is all about, the better.

"Have I organized my thoughts so that they're easy to follow?" Now is the time to juggle sentences around, putting related thoughts together in the same paragraph. Another way to make it easy for your reader is to do what both ad writers and textbook writers do: outline in "bullet" form, like this:

The three stages in the writing process are

- pre-writing or thinking
- rough draft
- revision.

"Is my tone right?" Read it out loud to see how it sounds. Is it stiff and pompous? harsh and angry? or worse, wishy-washy? You want to sound positive and self-confident: "I think this plan has great potential for . . ." is much more likely to get a positive reaction from your reader than, "The boss thought we should try this, so I'm running it by you to see . . ." The second example conveys the impression that you don't expect much. The reader won't either.

"Can I make it shorter?" You almost always can. Eliminate repeated thoughts; once is enough. Replace wordy phrasings, such as "It can be seen by the company that . . . ," with "The company sees . . ."; "at this point in time," with "now"; and "on account of the fact that . . . ," with "because." If your sentences ramble on and on, shorten them. Long, involved sentences are confusing to read.

"Have I told my reader what I want him/her to do?" A request for action often makes a good concluding sentence.

"Are spelling, punctuation, and grammar correct?" Correct any errors that you notice as you go along. Then, make one last careful check before the final typing, and if you've said what you have to say as simply and briefly as you can, your readers will be grateful. More importantly, they'll take action.

Look for good basic books on writing in the back of this book.

Despite the paraphernalia of dressing, thinking, and living for success and the battery of self-help manuals designed to help an employee improve his or her image and attitude on the job, it's vital to remember that employment is a contract that is honored by performance. Notwithstanding mentions of morale and Quality Circles à la Japanese industry, managers should concern themselves with those changes in behavior that make employees more effective.

American industry's renewed drive toward increased productivity makes individual performance reviews especially critical today. They are a good method for discovering who the company's high achievers are, rewarding them, and retaining them. Performance reviews are a valuable career tool for you because they can result in advancement, merit pay increases, and a future of increased responsibility and productivity. What's more, they are one of the best on-the-job learning situations you can have.

The best preparation for a review is to know precisely what your supervisor is going to evaluate. Both of you should agree—well in advance of the review—what your job actually entails and on what factors your performance is being judged. Get these down on paper, and, if possible, get a feeling for how important each is. The actual points will differ from organization to organization but are likely to include productivity, attitude, accuracy, reliability, and so on. Try to learn, in advance, the specifics *your* supervisor uses to measure these general points.

Make certain you know when your review will be held. If you know it is scheduled for three months from today, you have a target date by which you can bring all your assignments up to date and also psyche yourself up. One valuable asset when coming into the review is a working log. You can begin right now to keep a log that will tell your supervisor not just work assigned and completed, but any additional responsibilities you have volunteered to undertake or were assigned. It should also include those reasons (easily forgotten) why some assignments were late, why others went wrong. Having such data at your fingertips makes the whole thing easier to deal with.

During the review, try to remember that your supervisor has a certain investment in seeing that you do well. If you don't look good, it reflects on the person who hired you and who oversees your progress. And chances are, your supervisor knows a lot about your job and about what can be considered a reasonable level of productivity for it. So think of your reviewer as an instructor, or a counsellor, not a prosecuting attorney.

While you're being reviewed, try to learn. Concentrate on understanding what your appraiser is saying. Ask questions, or paraphrase his or her comments: "In other words, you want me to give you a report on this program the Friday after I get each assignment." Or, "You're saying, aren't you, that I should raise my typing speed to sixty-five words before my next review?" Ideally your supervisor will concentrate more on future performance than on past mistakes.

Discussing your shortcomings on the job is the part of the review that may be painful and that may lead to trouble. At this point, if you become instantly hostile or defensive, you won't be able to listen carefully to constructive criticism. Try to avoid personal remarks, lengthy explanations, and justifications in favor of the problems you and your supervisor face. If you blow up, your appraiser may wonder if you can handle the job professionally. So, if you feel yourself losing control, try to remember to say, "Look, I'm pretty upset about this. Can we talk it through tomorrow, after I've had a chance to think things out?" By the time you've cooled off, you may even have come up with a solution to the problem. But losing your temper at the wrong time might mean you lose your job, too.

Throughout the review, you and your appraiser should try to be as specific as possible. In that way you can brainstorm together and come up with solutions to your problems.

So try to get an exact description of where you fall short of requirements. ("You are producing only five units an hour, and we require a production rate of eight units to rate you excellent.") Once you come up with a standard of productivity, you and your appraiser can devise ways of meeting it. Try to set up a definite date by which you will have implemented these strategies, as in "six months from now at my next review, I will have learned not only to operate the word processor without supervision, but I will be studying one high-level computer language."

Once the review is over, find out your evaluation, and get it in writing. Never sign a blank review form. If you're doing well, keep it up. If you're in trouble, expect to receive written notice of each example of unacceptable behavior. If you're improving on some aspects of your job, try to get your supervisor to recognize your new behavior patterns and supply feedback. Look upon improvement as a cooperative procedure.

But let's assume the worst happens, and you are getting reviews you don't consider fair. Think them over. Talk about them with your reviewer. Then try to respond both orally and in writing before a third party—perhaps a personnel manager, or a company ombudsman. If your company has a union, you can take the matter up with your grievance committee. Let your supervisor know; nothing is more unproductive than going over his or her head. You will find that most companies are willing to resolve review problems promptly and fairly, especially if the employee making the complaint is productive. So while you're filing a grievance, don't pull a work slow-down. If your supervisor is unfair, slowing down will only provide more ammunition.

Today supervisors have one more reason to be especially fair to employees: companies are putting employees in the reviewer's role. Many forward-thinking organizations are developing and using anonymous questionnaires by which supervisors can be evaluated. If your company has such an arrangement, remember your supervisor is just as anxious about evaluation as you are. So apply the golden rule: review your supervisor the way you'd like to be reviewed yourself—calmly, clearly, and with an eye to on-the-job goals. After all, the person who will benefit most from your supervisor's improved performance is you.

The point of job reviews is to upgrade productivity, not to downgrade you. Regard your review as an analysis of strengths and weaknesses and a way of increasing your productivity. Do so and you've mastered an important career tool for making yourself a more valuable employee.

5
Getting Your Act Together

What is your personal work style? That's important; after all, to your boss, you *are* how you work. In order to put yourself on the fast track and stay there, the wise man or woman considers a variety of factors. Take job mobility. Almost no one really believes anymore that the only reliable employee is the forty-year veteran, but sometimes it's hard to distinguish between job-hopping and the proper time to switch.

Today's workplace is being changed by new technological advances: increasingly, these new, high technology industries and the demand for more savvy, better educated managers are producing a new breed. How is this new breed doing? Are you one of them? In that case, you might like to see how you're measuring up.

But developing an effective work style—for subordinate or manager—involves more than education or long-range planning. Once again, it's part of working smarter and more creatively, setting priorities and keeping to them. It's even the way you dress.

The smallest things, like neatly stacked papers on your desk or polished shoes, make a difference. *Remember the details.* They're a subtle, but important, part of your work style.

Lisa S. was on top of the world. Two months before graduation, and she'd already accepted a very flattering job offer from the marketing department of a major corporation. One afternoon, however, she got a long-distance phone call that shattered her plans. Department cutbacks had eliminated her position. Now what was she going to do?

Or take the case of Raymond J. For ten years he'd taught high school math until the defeat of three successive school levies forced his district to lay off 1,000 teachers. Despite tenure and all the talk about how the town needed good math teachers, Raymond found himself out of work. Did he have a right to be bitter?

And then there was Elaine B. Returning to work as a secretary after her children were in school, she handled correspondence for a man who dealt with many nurses, placing them on a permanent or temporary basis. When she wanted more money and autonomy than she was getting on the job, she looked around for the next step. It wasn't hard to find. Today, Elaine B. is the successful owner of an employment agency for nurses that places temporary workers nationwide.

Certainly, Elaine's case is clear-cut. She took certain skills she had gained in school, put them to work, and used her work time to observe how she could develop as a worker and, ultimately, as a manager. She planned, bided her time, gained necessary skills, and when she was ready, moved on. What's the next step for her? "Branch agencies, of course," she smiled.

But what about Lisa and Raymond? Like Elaine, they did everything right: got the proper training, worked hard, impressed interviewers, and, in Raymond's case, did well on the job. Yet they found themselves caught in the double bind of today's new job mobility.

For Lisa, a solution wasn't especially pleasant, but it was simple. She reported to her college placement office, began interviewing with companies, and sending her résumé out nationwide. Unfortunately, since she'd withdrawn her application from a number of places after accepting the job that had fallen through, she found she'd missed out on several opportunities. Since time was short, Lisa laid her plans carefully. She spent that summer (which she'd planned to enjoy travelling across the country) working as a temp in order to save enough money to finance an intensive full-time job campaign which ultimately produced several good offers. Today, says Lisa, "I'll never let myself be put in that position again." As a would-be marketing executive, Lisa is "positioning" herself always to have a back-up position. How? She has become active in local politics, participates in professional organizations, and has made the acquaintance of several recruitment firms. Even though she likes her present job and doesn't plan to switch, when her recruiter friends call with news of other positions, she listens. "After all," she concludes, "the best time to job-hunt is while you're already employed."

Raymond, the math teacher, found himself on the job market with teaching skills and a degree in mathematics. For awhile he found his job search hindered by one major factor: he was bitter, and it showed. Interviewers found him either pushy or apologetic. Finally one levelled with him, and Raymond realized that the time had come to change. He sat down with paper and pencil, and began to consider his options. What was he best at? Math. What else was he good at? Working with people; learning; applying for competitive programs. From talking with former colleagues, which required him to swallow some of his hostility and false pride, Raymond learned that his state and several major companies had instituted a program to retrain laid-off teachers as computer programmers. Raymond applied. His math skills, teaching experience, and ability to communicate won him a place in the program. Today, he is a systems analyst for one of the companies that sponsored the retraining program; moreover, several nights a week, he teaches computer programming at the local Y.

What do these three people have in common besides success? Each one of them faced situations which might have kept them feeling like losers or trapped in circumstances they didn't have a share in creating. Each legitimately could have felt mistreated, Lisa because a good job evaporated, Raymond because he was laid off, Elaine because she didn't have the power she would have liked in her first job. But each managed to overcome his or her feelings of being trapped or cheated and go on from there.

Now that each one is a success, however, it's interesting to note that not one of them is content with resting on past achievements. Lisa, Raymond, and Elaine are all planning for two things: the next step or the proverbial rainy day. At the foundation of these contingency plans is savings. "I like to have a couple month's pay in the bank," says Raymond. "That way, in case I have to look for a job, at least I've got time to do it in."

For Lisa, since she's only a few years out of school, further education is important. Since her company pays for work-related courses, she is taking graduate business training at night. And Elaine is going to buy a microcomputer to help herself keep track of her nurses and billing records. If her business expands, she'll need the computer for more complex record keeping. And if it doesn't? "In that case, I'll simply have to get a job programming for a hospital," she says.

You can use the above examples to plan your own career mobility. Not only should you research the field you're planning to enter, but you should keep tabs on your present and future jobs. Don't regard the simple fact of having a job as grounds for letting this research program, as well as your personal career planning, slide. And always have contingency plans: What happened to Lisa and Raymond can happen to you, too.

Notice, also, that these three individuals only switched jobs when they had to. Lisa and Raymond had no choice; Elaine moved on when she'd absorbed all that she could learn at her old job. But now that Lisa and Raymond are both employed, would they move on rapidly?

Possibly not. Their experiences have taught them several things: the importance of flexibility, having back-up plans, and the difference between job-hopping and job-jumping.

What is that difference? Job-hoppers change jobs at short intervals and for little reason. They get bored, possibly fired; they look around for a bit, and then land another job with approximately the same salary, duties, and responsibilities as the last one. Job-jumpers, on the other hand, look before they leap. They make lateral moves within a company or leave it for another company. But by and large, job-jumpers only jump when offered increases in responsibility, new skills, or good pay raises. For example, Lisa will only move now if a company offers her the jump from assistant account executive to account exec, with assistants under her. Raymond has no desire at all to leave his company, but he's beginning to consider switching to another division. Elaine, as proprietor of her own business, simply plans to expand.

How can you be a job-jumper, not a job-hopper? Follow these three short rules.

- In general, don't move unless you get more money. It's just as easy to work for a good salary as for peanuts.
- Watch your timing and your attitude. Don't switch jobs too often, and don't badmouth your last one. The work grapevine being what it is, job-switchers and gripers become known.
- Take stock of your career path, and progress regularly.

When trying to preserve your career mobility, the most important thing to remember is forcthought. Plan ahead, because careful planning will not only help you develop job-related skills but also keep your confidence up: After all, you *know* what you're doing, don't you? And, if you're flexible enough to acquire new skills and adapt to new situations, you have a good idea of what and who you are—valuable employee material. This will communicate itself to the interviewer who's sitting across from you. Good planning will not only keep you mobile but intensely marketable.

On the Launching Pad: You and Your Hi-Tech Future

The man who services your company's copiers, the real estate broker who has transferred records of apartments for rent into a database management system, the college junior majoring in computer science—

What do these people have in common? Simply this: They're all putting today's need for technology to work for them. In the next few years, a shift already present in the American work force is bound to widen the gap between people who are able to adapt to the growing "technologization" of the American workplace and those who are not.

In other words, the repairman who won't learn new systems, the secretary who doesn't learn word processing, the engineer who refuses to become computer-literate, and even the manager who shrinks from reading computer printouts will be competing for a shrinking pool of jobs.

So you can see there are decided advantages to "thinking hi-tech." If you're in school now (in which case, congratulations for reading this and planning in advance for your work life), your solution is simple. Consider majoring in one of the high-demand (and high-reward) technical fields such as computer science. Or, if you don't wish to major in such a field, consider taking at least one computer course. You may, of course, have no choice; many major universities are moving to make quantitative reasoning and programming part of their required curricula.

If you're working now, naturally you want to consider how you, too, can fit into the growing group of technologically literate workers.

How can you go about it? In the first place, remember this: Just because you want to become computer-literate or because you wish a career in a hi-tech company doesn't mean you have to become an engineer, a programmer, or, as many people seem to fear, some sort of mathematical genius. Unless you make them so, there is nothing intrinsically more intimidating about high-technology equipment than about forklifts, harvesters, or car engines. Consider the wide range of jobs available in high-technology firms, which require technical writers, service technicians, computer operators, sales representatives, computer-literate personnel executives, to name only a few employee groups, as well as computer programmers, analysts, and systems engineers.

If you want to retrain for a career in a high-technology firm, you should begin by finding a way to get further training: from a math-anxiety workshop for people truly afraid of working with hard data, to going back to school on company time (check your benefits pamphlet or speak to someone in your company's personnel department), to learning to use the word processor after hours. You might start reading up on advances in computer technology and maybe even get a home computer of your own.

The most important adaptation you can make in your work behavior is in your attitude—being willing and able to deal with change when it involves advanced new working tools and modes. Larry M., for example, refused to join his coworkers around the water cooler in their daily gripe sessions about the company's decision to install an electronic mail system. After all, they said, what was wrong with the old system, in which they handwrote their memos, then gave them to secretaries to type and distribute? It was a pain in the neck to learn the new electronic mail program, and they felt stupid every time they made mistakes. Not Larry, however; he became fascinated with the new mail system's possibilities. Soon he became known as the one person everyone went to when they had problems with the mail. He became responsible, at first unofficially, then officially, for training new employees in its use and serving as a liaison between his section and Data Processing. And then, when several of the secretaries complained of persistent headaches from using their terminals all day, he was an ideal choice to investigate the problem and help find a solution. Naturally this activity brought him to the attention of management, which responded with a raise and new responsibilities.

As Larry discovered, the new work aristocracy is going to be technologically literate. In the coming generation, the fast career tracks will be occupied by people who can function within a work world of computers, interactive terminals, executive work stations, dedicated data networks, word processing, automatic testing, and new computer and telecommunications-based ways to learn.

The switch to high-technology careers is something that not only you as a worker or student should consider, but also something that you should recommend to younger people. How can you get the next generation of workers intrigued with new technologies? If you're a parent, try buying a home computer; or, if that's prohibitively expensive, try urging your son or daughter to enroll in a high school computer club. Consider using your home video entertainment equipment as a way of intriguing your children with high technology. A really creative child might think of becoming a games designer or systems analyst, while someone more interested in taking the equipment apart and putting it back together might consider a future as a technician.

What if you're a teacher? First, you have an obligation to help steer your students in the direction of satisfying future careers. Secondly, you have an opportunity to influence them by example. Why not enter a computer course yourself and share your enthusiasm with your students? Leave copies of computer or games-related magazines around your classroom or order them for the library. Become involved in after-school related activities, such as computer clubs. And don't sneer at the kids who spend part of their lunch money on video games: They're not just playing; they're learning an ease and familiarity with software and computer graphics that you may envy later on.

Do you have to be an engineer or computer scientist to be computer literate these days? No more than you have to be a Pulitzer-Prize-winning novelist to write a good business letter. There is a place for you in high-technology industry; you have only to look for it.

With everybody talking career mobility, you may be wondering where it intersects your career goals. The mobile careerist expects to do a certain amount of moving around in the march toward those all-important career objectives.

If you're aiming for a high-level corporate job, use mobility to advance your career, suggests a vice-president of an international management consulting firm. Mobility within the organization can be easier and less risky, but it doesn't always work. For example, women who earn $40,000 or more annually and rank as vice-presidents of giant corporations apparently have consciously avoided the tenure trap. In general, the more highly compensated the woman officer, the shorter her sojourn has been with individual employers. Many observers believe the same is true of men.

So how do you increase *your* options?

As recently as ten or fifteen years ago, the answers to this question would probably have included such conventional attributes of success as performance, attitude, leadership ability, desire for responsibility, knowledge and experience, and initiative. Now the focus has shifted. Recent studies identify other factors that seem to propel the upward-bound.

True, not everyone in the work force is qualified to be or even *wants* to be a corporate vice-president. A grandson of the Ford Motor Company family recently announced his intention to remain in his present position, where presumably he's found satisfaction and challenge, rather than move up in the company. But the rules of the high flyers' game will help anyone who wants to move *up*, particularly if that person is also willing to move *around*.

1. *Job counseling.* Are you in the right field to start with? Where should you be heading? Good counselling is hard to find—and there are dubious organizations in this area; but searching for reliable advice can pay off. This is especially true now, when rapid changes are occurring; the career goals we adopted earlier in life may be obsolete, and many experts expect multi-career work styles to be the norm.

2. *A mentor.* Experienced bosses and coworkers who take younger employees under their wings, show them around, care, sponsor, criticize, share wisdom, and bestow blessings, offer both tactical and psychological value, say observers.

3. *Image.* How you dress, the impressions you project when you speak—almost everything about you—can help or hinder your upward mobility. Here, too, you need good advice, both from books on the subject and from counsellors or mentors.

4. *Willingness to take a risk.* Many people stay in dead-end jobs because they're afraid to change. Look for something that interests you—that's the key. Seek out the interesting exciting job or field that will stimulate you to perform at top level.

5. *Long hours and hard work.* The best advice to those who want to move up the ladder is, "Work at it." The most successful are not always the smartest. Instead they may be the ones who worked hard and made the extra effort. Others declare that the more time they devote to their work, the more money they'll make. Those earning over $40,000 average fifty-seven hours a week.

6. *Professional excellence.* A recent study uncovered a definite correlation between professional excellence and earning power. Academic excellence, extensive training, and advanced degrees are helpful in getting positions; but a consistent record of high achievement, job after job, is what can move you ahead.

7. *A purposeful attitude.* Again and again the quality of purpose turns up in studies of what makes people successful. Purpose and dedication are closely related. Both help you achieve the focus you need to succeed.

8. *Communication skills.* It's impossible to overrate the value of being able to communicate on paper and in front of people. In every aspect of business and corporate life, the biggest roadblock is failure to communicate clearly. Become a communicator and your success is virtually assured.

9. *Flexibility/adaptability.* One of the things that holds us back, say career counsellors, is that we get really rigid in our expectations. We need to be able to say, "Sure, I'll try it," and follow up by redirecting our energies, refocusing our sense of power. Flexibility is a quality well worth cultivating.

10. *Self-marketing.* We should all know how to "market" ourselves, in order to make our abilities and achievements clear to those who can help us reach career goals. Again, there are a number of books on the subject that you should seek out if, like many people, you find it difficult to "sell yourself." They will tell you it is not a matter of a glib pitch on how good you are that works, but being able to communicate examples of what you've done in your career that relate to your audience's own interests.

Minding Job Ps and Qs (Priorities & Quotas)

After some exposure to journalism and school publications, Marcia found a job with a small-town newspaper. Arriving at her desk promptly at 8:00, she checks her "to-do" list, stars her three top priorities, and

tackles the first one: sending bills to out-of-town subscribers. By 10
A.M., when she's written up a wedding and the church news, she's helping Jodie with the classifieds. Targeting priorities helped Marcia graduate in the top twenty-five percent of her class; for her it's the best way to
get things done.

Hal manages a small hardware store. With bike season approach-
ing, he needs to assemble and display a dozen or more racing and moto-
cross models. When the store is busy, he's lucky to get one bike a day
assembled and into the show window. If he can't do better, he'll lose
sales to the chain store down the street. Hal's solution: He set a quota—
two bikes a day before he goes home. Applying self-discipline to his
quota will boost his bike sales fifteen percent over this time last year.

Workers who care about their jobs are discovering new techniques
for getting things done. Priorities and quotas help them manage their
work load more efficiently. The result can be increased productivity,
recognition from superiors, and a satisfying sense of accomplishment.

Setting priorities forces us to evaluate tasks on the basis of importance and tackle them accordingly. It also forces us to make decisions
about what *not* to do. Do you consciously select the most important
priority or do you fall into the path of the most interesting one?

One help in "prioritizing" is the to-do list. At the end of the working day, jot down a list of things you need to do tomorrow. Next morning, evaluate these tasks; target the most important and tackle them
first.

Understandably, differing perceptions of what's important can
lead to conflicts. Janet discovered the engineers in her department gave
their own projects a high priority. Janet's job is to operate word processing equipment, not make critical decisions about whose work comes
first. Her solution? She asks the engineers to number each project that
goes to her "in-box." If the last job was #107, the next is #108. Every job
gets done in that order unless the supervisor tags it "rush." Her boss's
comment: "It's unbelievable how effective this system is and how
many hassles it prevents."

Some people base priorities on order of importance; others wait
until a situation becomes urgent before attending to it. Still others
work to deadlines: If a report is due May 1, Hector gets started April 1,
aiming to have it done by the 20th.

Similar to goals, quotas are usually characterized by numbers
specifying some share or allotment. In her job with an electronics assembly firm, Kay is given a production quota based on average performance. If she slows down one day, she can speed up the next and still
meet the quota. If she consistently beats it, she gets a quarterly production bonus.

However, setting our own quotas instead of having others do it for
us gives us the good feeling of being in control. Your motivation will be
higher when you set your own quotas.

Want to put quotas to work for you? Consider these tips:

1. *Set quotas high enough to motivate you, but not too high.* (That could be a turn-off.) Leo is studying engineering drawing at the community college. Studying isn't all that easy. Leo's study quota? Thirty minutes in the morning before his noisy kids get up; thirty minutes more after they're in bed.

2. *Put quotas in writing.* Mark sells plumbing supplies. His company-set quota is $50,000 a week; his goal for himself: $60,000 in signed orders. With the "extra" money he makes, he and Leah can make a down payment on that acre near the lake.

3. *Reward yourself.* Gale's professional organization is trying to raise $5,000 for the new library. She accepted a quota of $500. She'll ring three doorbells or phones a day, until she can present pledges for the full amount to her team leader. Then she and her three-year old son will spend a whole day at the zoo. Setting quotas and using priorities can help you achieve your career goals and feel good while doing it.

Managing Your Paperwork

How often has this happened to you? A coworker stops by your office or workspace for a brief chat, perhaps to discuss a new project. He or she looks for a place to sit down and finds chaos. Immediately, you lift papers, notebooks, and reports off your extra chair. Finally your visitor sits down. Now, can you finally get down to work? Not until you've said what you've said a thousand times before: "Sorry that my desk is such a mess."

Very likely, your visitor's going to answer, "That's all right. You ought to see mine." But should you really need to apologize? And, much more importantly, should you need to apologize to your boss if he or she is the visitor? Granted, you know how easily you can turn that mass of papers, letters, documents, books, and reports (not to mention all those coffee cups) into productive material. After all, you've done it before. But if your boss sees it, it's possible that he or she may get the idea that a messy desk reflects its owner's work habits and thought patterns. And even if the boss doesn't reflect on it consciously, such a thought can be damaging to you when it's time to hand out promotions, evaluations, and recommendations.

But you know all that already. Doubtlessly you've come up with rationalizations for all the clutter. Here are two of the most common: "I'll stick all this stuff in the files." or, "No one will notice." Untrue. Buried files, as you've probably found out long before reading this, have a way of turning into precisely the files someone needs—right now. No one will notice? Not likely.

With the increasing automation in many offices, don't think you can escape the clutter of paperwork by putting everything into computer memory, or onto the word processor. Computer memories are finite. As for hard copy—it accumulates too. Haven't you seen the stacks and stacks of green-and-white printouts that clutter every available inch of desk, floor, and chair in some people's offices?

How can you manage your paperwork? The best way is to make a plan and follow it systematically. Tomorrow, plan to come in to work half an hour early. (Tempting as housekeeping on company time may be, it's not what you were hired to do.) Now, organize your papers into stacks: one stack for each subject or project. *Do not throw out a scrap* . . . yet. (Except, of course, all those old coffee cups and candy wrappers.) Now, examine each stack. Do you really need ten duplicates of that report? Carefully discard as many as you feel you must, but leave yourself a spare copy. Do not throw away typed or handwritten originals or notes.

That huge stack over on the corner of your desk is a report—several drafts of the report, to be exact. Have you labeled each draft clearly? Have you dated them? Do so; it'll help you keep track of your progress. Now clip the drafts and place them in a file marked with the subject of the report. If the report has been sent to typing, file the drafts away immediately. Correspondence next. Do you have copies of letters that are being mailed? Clip them to the letters they answered. If the correspondence relates to an ongoing project, attach it; otherwise, look for the correspondence file. If there isn't one, consider starting it.

Now look around. All those printouts—if you can't get rid of them, can't you at least stack them neatly? You could probably begin to arrange them systematically, while you're at it. And for the final, orderly touch: you've probably accumulated work materials that you don't need—your supervisor's handbook, your neighbor's technical publication, the stapler from someone else's desk. Return these things to their proper owners.

Next, sit down at your newly ordered desk. It's almost time to start work. In a few minutes, the first of today's epidemic of letters, memos, reports, requisitions, bills, and various other kinds of papers are going to land on your desk, transforming a now organized surface into a wood-pulp blizzard unless you figure out a system for handling your paperwork. First things first. Jot down a list; what's your first priority? Do you immediately receive your mail in the morning? In that case, there may be letters or bills you need to deal with immediately. Sort them out, then discard unnecessary "junk" mail. There's no point in wasting time over the circular offering you Florida real estate; everyone on your floor got one anyhow. Now that you've taken care of the important incoming mail, what about the outgoing mail? Some letters need to go out immediately; tend to them. Others can be postponed until later in the day.

What about the rest of your paperwork? Doubtless you're groaning. After all, you say, you were hired as an engineer, a librarian, a teacher, or whatever, not a paper-pusher. Still, there the stuff is, and it's got to be dealt with in addition to the job for which you were hired and which you really want to do. Sometimes it seems to be too much to cope with.

In general, the best way to allot time for this drudge work is to figure out your least productive moments and do it then. For example, if you know from experience that you're capable of working all morning without interruption, but that you begin to flag right before lunch, possibly you can deal with low-priority paperwork at that time. Another good time for it is in the half-hour before a meeting or before you take up a new task. And what about those snippets of time before you go home? Not only will tidying up stray paperwork and making certain that it's sensibly organized on your desk assure people that you're not a clock-watcher who's going to run out of the office at 5:00, but it'll get you started right for tomorrow's work too.

Now it's quitting time. All your paperwork is done and filed away in its proper place except for ongoing tasks. Before you leave, take out one last piece of paper and place it on the desk where you'll see it first thing tomorrow morning. On it jot down a list of the things you have to do tomorrow. Now you're prepared to spend tomorrow working smarter, without being inundated by paperwork.

New Insights on Women, Dress, and Business

Can a carefully chosen outfit, worn to that all-important first interview, clinch a particular job for the female applicant? Should a working woman expect to dress like a man to increase her chances of success in the business world? Must a woman give up her femininity and individuality for a place on the board of directors?

Ten years ago, questions like these would have elicited blank stares from personnel consultants and female job applicants alike. You wore your best clothes which, more often than not, were a combination of what was currently in style for daytime wear and what your pocketbook could bear. But the entry of record numbers of women into the business world and the increasing competition between men and women on all levels of responsible management, have forced management consultants, personnel administrators, and observers of the business scene to take a closer look at what women are wearing to work.

In a recent national survey of working women, conducted by a fashion magazine, 55 percent of the women surveyed said that clothes were an important part of their business image. But a whopping 70 percent also thought that femininity was important to their image as women. Is there a way to reconcile these two views?

Women in business may not find it easy to solve this dilemma, but how to dress in a "business uniform" is a step toward professional equality with their male counterparts. What will a woman look like if she dresses in the business uniform? A two-piece, conservatively styled suit (jacket and skirt) in a neutral color (no pink, red, yellow, or sky blue, please) is the favored look. No sweaters, no vests, and no skirts without matching jackets should be part of the businesswoman's professional wardrobe. Extremely fashionable clothes and summery sundresses are not considered serious enough for business wear. A briefcase completes the professional woman's image; the traditional carryall of women, the handbag, is frowned upon as too fussy. In short, the implication is that women have to imitate men to get ahead in business. To what extent is this really the situation?

How Personnel Directors See You.   A national fashion magazine decided to test some of these theories on how women should dress for business. They selected a variety of firms and sent them five photographs of the same woman, dressed in different outfits. At each firm, the personnel director was asked to evaluate the woman in the photograph as if she were present at an interview for a management trainee position. (They were also asked to assume she had the appropriate qualifications and credentials for the job.)

The results clearly indicated that employers wanted to recruit competent women who looked polished, but feminine. They emphatically did not want to hire carbon copies of businessmen. In fact, the photograph of the woman wearing a conservative, neutral-colored business suit and carrying a briefcase was rejected by almost all the firms as too severe and mannish. One personnel administrator claimed that this photograph projected an intimidating image and the model was probably an inflexible person. On the other hand, the photograph of a woman wearing the latest trends in fashion, including a frizzy hairdo, was also regarded suspiciously by almost all the firms. She was not considered management potential because she was dressed inappropriately, her hair looked unkempt, and she was thought to be wearing too much makeup.

The hands-down winner of the survey managed to combine the best of the business uniform with some feminine touches. The woman most likely to be hired wore a neutral-colored stylish suit, with a turtleneck sweater, fashionable shoes, and a leather shoulder-bag. She was described enthusiastically by personnel interviewers as smart, serious, and able to handle any event of the business day. By dressing carefully, she presented a self-assured and career-oriented image while enhancing her femininity. It was clear from the remarks of the personnel directors that the matching jacket projected an executive image.

How It Applies to You.   The moral of all this advice is this: If you are a woman preparing to get ahead in your chosen career, pay some attention to the clothing you wear.

There is no question that certain kinds of clothing are more appropriate for office surroundings. Research by social scientists has shown that people assume someone whose garb is attractive and well put together will perform better than someone who is not as well dressed. While no amount of taste and expensive clothing will cover a job that is done ineptly, a well-groomed, tailored image will probably help you feel good about yourself and help you do a good job at work. So if you are in the market for both a new job and a new suit, don't sacrifice femininity and taste for a passing fashion trend or a businessman's look-alike doublebreasted uniform.

6

Dilemmas
and Decisions

You've probably seen the sign tacked to someone's bulletin board. *Plan Ahead*! it says. But the last three letters are squeezed together to fit into too little space. An example, if ever there was one, of bad planning. All too often, people's work lives resemble that sign. Initially in control, they suddenly find themselves in a welter of unsolved tasks and time-consuming details they'd hardly planned on. The fact is, they hadn't planned at all, because they didn't know they had to.

Throughout your work life, you're going to be asked to make a variety of decisions. Some look relatively simple like learning to type. As too many women have discovered, typing can be the lock on the cage of a dead-end job. But it can also be the key to a bright future, an entry into the computer field in which typing is necessary in order to input information. It all depends on how you plan to use your skill. Or consider office politics. Haven't you ever wondered how the wheeler-dealer in the corner office got to sit there? Sure, you may not want to resemble that person, but do you want to be like the workaholic over in the shadows who barely smiles, works at least ten hours a day, and seems to have no life outside the job? And by the way, how do you work with a workaholic? That's a dilemma you may face. So is being one.

Or let's say you've decided to make a fresh start. You've moved to a new town, found a new job; *now* what do you do? For a start, read on.

Doing It on Your Own: Single People and Relocation

Once upon a time, when single people finished school, they stayed in or returned to their hometowns, got a job nearby, and eventually left home to get married. These days, singles move readily from small town to big city, from big city to small town, looking for a different life style, new opportunities, seeking the job they want or have trained for. While they don't have some of the relocation worries of marrieds—family disruption, mortgage costs, the two-career problem—they do encounter other problems. They, too, have to find places to live, jobs, social contacts, and make the adjustment to new living and working environments. Most singles do this alone, with little or no help in terms of finances, information, and the logistics of moving themselves and their possessions—the kind of help that most corporations these days automatically supply to both relocated employees or new hirees.

If you're about to become one of these relocating singles, therefore, without the support of a corporation, "the new girl/guy in town," here are some tips that may help you avoid the anxiety and upset that changes in one's life style inevitably bring:

- First, don't just pull up stakes and go without doing some advance planning. Arriving in a new locale is twice as hard when you don't know the territory. Get familiar with the area, read about it, ask around for anyone you may know who has lived there. Find out about the people and customs. Listen to some personal anecdotes to get the feel of the place.

- You can find out a lot about a town by reading the local newspaper. (You can find the paper's name and address at your public library, in the *Ayer Directory of Publications*.) Subscribe to the paper and to local magazines if they exist. Go to the library, too, for books on the area and especially look for books aimed directly at relocaters. There are a few now available that describe individual cities from the viewpoint of new arrivals.

- Then make up a pre-move checklist to determine the things you still need to know, including such practical points as what you can expect to pay for rent, the tax rates in the city and the state (if other than your own), neighborhoods to choose or avoid, and companies in the area where you might find a job. (You'll find these in the classified columns of the paper you've subscribed to.)

- Try writing to the Chamber of Commerce, the tourist bureau of larger cities and the town clerk of a small town, for information spelling out your special problems and needs. If it's a small city, register with several real estate or rental agencies. They often have extensive material on the area for their clients including area maps. (Ask the Chamber of Commerce for their names.) Banks sometimes sponsor newcomer programs like the one in a small midwestern city that provides a Newcomer Center which has all the things one needs to know about the town—housing, utilities and recreational information, drivers' manuals for out-of-staters, maps, and change-of-address kits. They also sponsor a free city tour and have a staff on hand for personal assistance on specific problems.

- You can get a more concrete idea of the ambiance of the place by actually going there and staying for a week or two on your vacation. This is good exposure to the realities and a potential way to acquire another important relocation asset—getting to know somebody who actually lives where you plan to move. In one case, for example, Jim G., from a small midwestern city, wanted to move to New York City. Through his only contact, a college friend, he got a summer rental of an apartment there. This provided the base for finding a job, a place of his own, and entry, as well, into a small network of friends.

- When it comes to arranging for the move, there are many places you can go for practical information. Most large moving companies have information services. Atlas Van Lines, for example, has a series of "how to" booklets with tips on moving practically anything from a plant to a pet. You'll find a local Atlas office in the phone book's Yellow Pages, or write to: Marketing Division, Atlas Van Lines, P.O. Box 509, Evansville, IN, 47703. The Office of Consumer Protection has a kit that includes a performance report on the nation's top movers. Ask for Public Advisory #4 from Office of Consumer Protection, 12th and Constitution Ave., NW, Washington, DC, 20423.

Moving into a big city from a small community is a tough and sometimes shocking experience. But moving from a large city to a small town has its own culture shock as well. After Robert H.'s Chicago apartment was burglarized for the third time, he jumped at a chance to move to a small Ohio city. But almost as soon as he unpacked his bags, plugged in his TV, and organized his books, he started to get depressed. Though the job he found was enjoyable, most of his coworkers were married and he had nothing to contribute to conversation about the PTA and crabgrass. He had fallen victim not only to "culture shock" but to post-moving letdown. The excitement of the adventure was gone, and the unfamiliar was strange and unsettling.

Bob worked his way out of this common relocation syndrome when he learned through a chance conversation that his company had a baseball team. This had always been a favorite sport, and he immediately joined the team. Sports, in turn, brought him into contact with a number of people who could see him now, not just as the worker in the next department, or a big city refugee, but as a fellow sports enthusiast and player. His desire to insulate his house before winter also brought him good advice from his new friends, as well as lots of free help and a housewarming party when the job was done. In a few months, he found that he had made the transition happily to a new life style.

You're lucky. As a single, you have access to a really broad range of options. You can probably choose the section of the country you'd like to live in, the type of environment—big city, small town, or rural community— and the kind of home you want—an apartment, condo, co-op, or even a house in some areas of the country. Take advantage of these options and follow your heart. You'll learn a great deal about people and different life styles than the one you grew up with as well as a lot about yourself.

Handling Those Sunday Night Blues

Some people say that the country music hit of the late 70's, "Sunday Night Blues," is really a theme song for a big percentage of the country's workers. Certainly it captured a much wider audience than is usual for such music.

Such blues afflict men and women who dread getting up Monday morning to go off to a job they dislike. And it may account for the fact that so many people today often change not only their jobs but their field of work as well in a continuing but generally futile search for satisfaction. There are jobs that are going to be dismal, no matter what; but sometimes people make their jobs unpleasant because of the attitudes they take toward them. If you've got the Sunday night blues, it may be possible to generate a change by giving some thought to your attitudes.

The Perfection Attitude. Some people are uptight before they get to the job because they're afraid of making mistakes. This happens to people who are particularly upset by criticism, for example, or who have had bad working experiences under bosses who get violently angry when mistakes occur. Then, some people have an image of themselves as being always right or feel insecure about holding the job (which heightens the pressures and can cause mistakes) or have other personal hangups along these lines.

It can help, if you are one of these people, to realize that doing a good job doesn't mean being right all the time. Nobody is. From the new employee on the assembly line to the president of the company, people make errors under the pressures of work. If you do make a mistake, your work life will be more comfortable if you admit it, learn from it, and take it in stride. Even if you get criticized, that means that you're regarded as somebody who can improve or else the effort wouldn't be made.

Avoid criticizing yourself to others, which some people do as a kind of penance for making a mistake. Such public self-criticism not only bores other people but, if done often, can give you an image as a loser even to yourself.

Depersonalizing Pressure. It's a rare job that doesn't involve the person doing it in a lot of pressure from time to time. One way you can make that aspect of your job easier to live with is to acquire the habit of depersonalizing the pressure when it comes.

Often job pressure comes from the person above you who may not be skilled in handling people or who may be under a lot of pressure that you aren't aware of. "Why did you do a thing like this?" is usually the gist of what's said, a question which in itself accuses you of deliberately doing the wrong thing. This can be handled, often, by speaking objectively rather than personally. Rather than saying, "I couldn't get the figures from the sources you gave me," which puts things on a personal level, say, "The figures were not available." This statement shifts the situation into neutral.

Another way of handling pressure, particularly when you feel you're going to make a strong emotional response, is to remove yourself from the situation for a short time. Who can question a trip to the rest room or the drinking fountain? Yet, having these few minutes gets your feelings under control, and collecting your thoughts can make a great deal of difference. Calming yourself can also help the people you work with deal more frankly with you, since you won't come on as oversensitive. It can even earn you a reputation for clear thinking.

Get the Picture. Psychologists say that part of the reason people get the Sunday night blues is that they literally don't know what they're doing: The work they and their section do is only one aspect of a much bigger job. If you're assembling a car or a piece of electronic equipment, you have an idea of the end product. But for many people, it isn't so clear cut.

One company that makes mine safety equipment recognized the problem and took groups of their workers to a distant coal mine where the people who actually made the equipment could see it in use and listen to miners tell them about its value and importance to their safety. The results were a dramatic change to positive feelings about the job and the products. The picture at your place of work may not be so dramatic, but if you are aware of how your effort fits in, not only in terms of the company but also the people who use the end product, work can be a lot more satisfying.

Maybe you're the one in your department who should start to find out more; your company is likely to cooperate.

Not by bread alone. The old saying about not living by bread alone also applies to work. You can deal better with a dull job if you have other things in your life that you're enjoying and that give your abilities an outlet: volunteer work, hobbies, sports, courses at night school, and so on. Channeling your energies and interests in other directions helps keep the inevitable frustrations and job pressures in perspective.

The Home Computer: a New Working Tool for You

For working at home, for starting your own business, or for getting ahead on your present job, you may have to join the computer generation via one of the new personal computers (PC's). These desk-top machines, scarcely larger than a typewriter, are being used by an increasing number of people to help streamline their busy lives. Paying bills, balancing checking accounts, keeping track of important dates, and home inventory control are some of the personal uses to which these fantastic little machines are now being put. But looming even larger for the future are the ways in which the home computer can be an important element in your working career.

Giant steps forward in technology now enable a small, personal computer to do the work of several employees. It can keep your files, write letters, make charts and graphs, do your bookkeeping, bill your customers, write your checks, keep your income/expense figures up to date, figure your taxes and payroll, bring you the latest stock market figures, tap data banks, and more.

A small contractor who has his office at home is now able to do job-costing and production-scheduling on his home computer. A young couple run a lucrative mail-order business using their PC to keep track of inventories and build up mailing lists. An architect in California works out of his home, without any office staff, using a computer which does his job estimates, bookkeeping, and filing. A doctor in San Francisco keeps all his insurance forms and patient files on his home computer.

A shortage of secretaries has created a new application for the home computer. Using word processor programs for their PCs, secretaries can work free lance in their homes part time or run a home typing business while they keep an eye on their homes and families.

The continuing shortage of programmers has opened up opportunities for computer work at home. Programmers, with their own sophisticated computers, can now work out programs to order for several companies on a free-lance basis, thus filling in vacant programmer slots for several companies at the same time. One expert has estimated there may be as many as 10,000 such independent programmers in the San Francisco Bay area alone.

But you don't have to be a free lancer or own a business to make your personal computer pay off. If you have a nine-to-five job and have your eye on the next step up the company ladder, a personal computer will allow you to do a high volume of "homework" fast, accurately, and efficiently or to do your job in new ways. Allen, a young junior executive, invested in his own computer and worked out market projections for his company's product line on his own at night. An impressed management responded with a raise and a promotion. One ad executive carries a briefcase-sized computer to meetings with clients and dazzles them with on-the-spot ad budget computations.

How to Choose a Computer   There are more and more different kinds of computers becoming available—a veritable menu of computers designed to fill an expanding array of information processing needs. Many people are bewildered by the maze of options open to them. But if looking into your own future, you feel that working at home via computer may be for you, now is a good time to begin investigating what is available and how it can serve your needs. There's more help around than you may think. Begin by

1.   *enrolling in a short course in "computer literacy"* given locally by adult education centers or by business people as one-day seminars. These courses do not teach programming. They *do* teach you the jargon, show you what a computer can do for you, and clue you in on what to look for when you talk to salespeople. Look for these courses advertised in the business pages of your newspaper or contact your local community college or adult evening school.

2.   *seeing personal computer demonstrations.* You probably need go no farther than your local shopping mall. The Tandy Corporation retails its line of computers through 8,000 Radio Shack stores worldwide. Computerland is a leading computer retail chain offering many brands with 250 stores in the U.S. Recently Sears, Roebuck & Company announced plans to open computer stores in a few cities on a trial basis. Many other stores are servicing this new field.

Don't be shy about asking questions. It's a new field, and most people are unschooled in this most recent advance in technology. It's a great chance to learn, and the stores are eager to give you all the help they can.

3.   *knowing what you want your computer to do for you* and searching for the machine that can do it. What one make doesn't have, for example, portability, another will. And remember you are not just buying a piece of equipment, like a typewriter or a calculator. Each computer has the capacity to use many predesigned programs that give it certain talents, such as figuring taxes or market strategies, collating information, keeping accounts. But these programs often fit only the computer for which they were written. So check to see what programs are available for each computer you consider for present use as well as for the future.

4.   *checking out its expandability.* Be sure to take into consideration the likelihood of more programs becoming available, the possibility of expanding your computer rather than buying a second one later, and the available auxiliary equipment.

How Much Will a Home Computer Cost?   Typical computers for home use now cost as little as $600. The more complicated your needs, the more you'll need to pay. But you can generally start with a less expensive model and add additional capabilities later.

In addition to the basic machine, you may need "peripherals" or "software"—other machines that add to its flexibility.

For example, if you want your computer primarily to turn out written material, you'll need a word processing program (the software) and a printer (the hardware). Printers run from several hundred dollars to as much as the computer itself. Some programs come with the computer, but for additional programs you may pay up to a hundred or more dollars each.

If you want to "talk" to other computers via the telephone lines, the modem which allows that is another extra. (Though, if you're doing free-lance work at home, it may be paid for by the company you're working for.)

Where Can I Get More Information?   Whatever your plans for joining the computer revolution, keep in mind that it's happening so fast that information is outdated almost as fast as it is written. Some recent information to give you background in computers will be found under sources at the back of this book.

Typing: Key(board) to Your Future?

"Never admit that you know how to type . . ." and "You can always fall back on typing if you have to . . ." are two common and conflicting pieces of advice that arc taking on new meaning in the 80's. When the typewriter was first introduced, most typists were male, because it was thought that the machinery was too complicated for women to use. This changed to the point that most typists were women, and typing ability often meant consignment to a dead-end job in the typing pool. Came the women's rights movement and the opening of new kinds of jobs and the typewriter became the symbol of "office slavery"— something the person who wanted to get ahead should avoid.

Now, however, we're in the middle of another major change in which the ability to work with a keyboard can be a very positive asset to your future in a number of ways. Typing is literally the key to the "office of the future." It can open up new careers for you and influence your performance and achievement at any number of jobs right on up to the executive suite.

Ways Mastering the Keyboard Can Help You

1. *Working at Home.* In university towns the going rate for typing a term paper is high. Typing manuscripts and reports is being used by many people in these locations, including women with young children and handicapped persons, as a way to make a living without having to leave home.

Now this idea is being extended by some banks and businesses, who are farming out not just typing but word processing and even computer programming (which also requires knowledge of the typing keyboard) to people who perform these jobs in their own homes. One thing making this possible is that these new machines can be hooked up so that work is delivered electronically to the company.

2. *Typing and Temporaries.* The temporary help field is distinctly a growth industry. If you're a competent typist, it offers you cash, experience, and a foot in many company doors. One of Manpower's offices in an eastern location reports typists can earn over $6.00 an hour, for example, depending on experience, ability, and how they rank on the company's specialized tests. Rates vary by geographic region and individual skill, of course, but even light typing skills in a small town can mean $3.35 an hour, says a representative from Kelly Services. If you become a highly trained word processor, that rate could go up to over $12.00 per hour.

The Word Processing Boom.   The rapid spread of word processing machinery is creating considerable demand for people who can do this more highly skilled work. Interestingly enough, history seems to be repeating itself in a small way. According to the president of one personnel service firm, half the people learning word processing at his company's training center are men. His organization charges several hundred dollars for a course in the field, which suggests what you might have to invest to acquire this new skill.

Alternatives are available, of course, including on-the-job training, training at a school run by a company that manufactures such equipment, local adult education courses in your community, and so on. In some areas word processor rates for temporaries are reported to run from $7.00 to $11.00 an hour during days, occasionally up to $25.00 for night or week-end duty. One manager of temporary workers in New York reports that in a recent year an enterprising word processor earned over $30,000 working the midnight to 8 A.M. "graveyard shift."

Typing and a Professional Career. As already noted, being able to use a keyboard is basic to such data processing professionals as programmers and systems analysts. In many fields today, particularly information-oriented ones such as journalism, publishing, advertising, and so on, good typing is a necessity, and more and more portable word processing machines are being utilized.

For numbers-oriented fields—business, accounting, insurance, banking—entering information into a computer's memory banks and calling it up again, requires the ability to use the video display terminal's typewriter-like keyboard.

This trend will be accelerated as office automation proceeds at full speed, since it is based on the handling and transfer of information typed into various data processing and word processing machines. Consequently the stereotype of the business executive at a paper-cluttered desk dictating to his/her secretary is a rapidly fading image. A more accurate picture is an executive typing at his or her video display terminal to obtain, organize, and transmit information throughout the company.

One portent of this is the vast number of management people who have already acquired "personal" computers, which they bring to their desks and then take home to do both business and personal paperwork.

If, for many years, the question, "Can you type?" signified a career detour for many able and ambitious women, the question today—for both men and women—takes on new meaning. That sometimes maligned ability can put you in the mainstream of business and open many career doors.

Making a Five-Year Plan

Rebecca A. loved the creativity and variety of her job as a children's book editor with a small Minneapolis publishing firm.

But after five years, her salary was only $10,000—hardly commensurate with her college degree and experience. The possibilities for promotion were slim since family members of the firm's owners held key jobs.

When she asked herself where she'd be in another five years, she saw a dead-end sign. Today, she works as a public relations officer for a Minnesota power company. Designing brochures and writing articles fulfills her creative urges, her salary has doubled, and the promotion potential is high.

Admitting she sounds a little like a Soviet economist, Rebecca is one year into what she calls her five-year plan.

"I just realized that if I wanted to get somewhere in my career I'd have to start planning," she explains. The next step is for her to attain a supervisory position in the public relations department.

College placement directors, company personnel officers, and employment agency managers agree that making a five-year plan is a good way for an employee with ambition to clarify goals. If you aren't heading in the direction of your five-year goal, they warn, it's time to switch directions.

Be realistic, they add, but don't be so afraid of losing job security that you won't take a chance that could greatly enhance your career.

Michael Weldon, president and general manager of Management Recruiters, emphasizes that the first thing you must do is ask yourself what you're qualified to do. Be realistic. Maybe you *want* to be a professional guitarist, but if you earned a degree in engineering and the last time you played guitar was back in high school, you'd better think twice, or maybe three times.

Weldon believes that companies are more eager to hire a person who knows what his or her goals are than someone who is uncertain. If you are ambitious, he cautions, look for a company that offers on-the-job training or reimbursement for tuition; promotion potential because it seeks people to promote within the company rather than bringing in supervisors from outside; and a top-line benefits package.

Many people who are dissatisfied with the direction their careers are taking mistakenly think an advanced degree will open doors for them, Weldon comments. Though graduate degrees and vocational education can be very helpful, Weldon says, he urges the would-be student to study the value of the degree very carefully before he goes back to school.

"An MBA (Master of Business Administration) is considered a hot degree now. Some guy may read in the paper that an MBA will get him a $45,000-a-year job, even without experience. Well, that's really not true unless that person goes to an Ivy League school and gets a job with a top company."

A professor of journalism who also serves to place journalism graduates in jobs agrees with Weldon that many graduate students undertake advanced degrees without much forethought about marketing them afterward. According to him, they just decide they want to go back to school. And as many people have discovered, being a "perpetual student" isn't going to help you with the personnel screeners.

This professor thinks that even recent college graduates can easily get into a job rut. He tends to contact students after they've been out working for about five years. Generally, he finds that a good time to see how they're doing and to advise them of new job possibilities. Generally he finds that students have settled in. Generally they've married, bought a house, started a family, and put down roots. They don't want to move. They're probably romanticizing both their first jobs and their loyalty to their employer. But give them five more years, and they may be restless. Then, however, it's harder for them to move on because there will be fewer positions at their level of responsibility. They won't be locked in but they're not as mobile as they were. And young professionals need to stay mobile.

A nationally known career counselor and author, John Crystal, recently said in a newspaper interview that job candidates should ask themselves, "what kind of life do I want?" before they ask themselves "what kind of job can I get?"

So when you're looking for a job, decide how you want to live. See if the area you think you'd like to live in offers you work and recreational facilities in order to live the way you want. Define your goal first and work backward.

Jack L., a young businessman, recently took that advice. Since being self-employed has always been his ideal, an inexperienced Jack started his own small advertising business as soon as he graduated from college. After several years of ups and downs, critical problems in meeting the payroll, and replacing cancelled accounts, Jack realized he should learn the ropes working for someone else before striking out on his own again. Several months of searching provided just the right job in the promotion department of an established company.

What about that dream of owning his own business?

Jack's grin shows he learned the hard way when he answers, "That's the goal of the five-year plan."

Do You Know a Work Junkie?

Do you know people who simply cannot stop working, no matter how hard they try? These people can't help it—they become restless and feel they must report to work early, stay late, work week-ends, and shun vacations. It could be your spouse, colleague, friend, or boss, possibly even yourself, who qualifies as a workaholic.

Workaholics, described in a recently published book on the subject as "work junkies . . . they are addicted to their jobs," are sought by some employers for their energy and drive and treated by some psychiatrists for their inability to relax. The subject has received wide attention.

Workaholics are motivated by the drive to do more and more work, not just gain a raise or promotion. They exist in every occupation, among both sexes, and across the country—not just among the highly paid executives or professionals but also among production workers.

How can a person who punches a time clock be a workaholic? Even if overtime is not approved, he or she may come in early, then punch in at the regular starting time.

There are and have always been women workaholics. Look at generations of compulsive houseworkers, who clean twenty-four hours a day . . . including weekends. Or organizers of charity events who drive themselves to exhaustion.

Workaholics, contrary to popular mythology, are not always unhappy. Many are successful in every sense of the word, living full and satisfied lives.

And it would appear that workaholics start to develop young. They sell more Girl Scout cookies, Christmas cards, and magazine subscriptions than anyone else on the block. They race home from school to do their homework, and then work on "extra credit" projects. The young workaholic may see his/her achievements as necessary for parental love and become afraid of failure.

What if a workaholic wants to learn to relax, to take vacations, and enjoy leisure time? Various types of psychotherapy have been used successfully with workaholics who wish to slow down, including one psychiatrist who takes his workaholic patients hiking and another who sees such patients on his yacht.

What are the lessons to be learned from workaholics? On the negative side, workaholics have usually not learned that by delegating and sharing work, the job can be accomplished with less strain. Workaholics, also, tend to be perfectionist beyond the necessity of the task. On the positive side, life can be more interesting if we don't shut ourselves off from thinking creatively about our jobs after work hours.

OPTIONS AND DIRECTIONS

Many people have a cut-and-dried view of work and the workplace: nine to five; an office, either in a small, mom-and-pop company or in a big, impersonal one; a noisy production line; five days a week; two weeks and major holidays off. It's no wonder that such people find their work lives humdrum. They haven't kept up with the changes that are taking place both on the job and in the way people look at work. Consequently, any suspicions they have that they're being left behind are probably right.

What causes people to act and think this way? They're bound by "traditional wisdom," the sort that preaches how to succeed in terms of fifty years ago.

But if you examine what such people take for granted, you're likely to come up with a number of questions. Why shouldn't you work at home? If you can work two jobs, why not? If a part-time job will pay your bills, is there anything wrong in just working part-time? Not at all. What if you get easily bored? Instead of trying to adjust to the same employer and surroundings, day in and day out, why not become a "full-time temp?"

And then there are the basic changes made in today's work by the intrusion of new fields, such as high-technology industry, for which "tried and true" work patterns just may not be effective. Another revolutionary change: the altered expectations of working women.

This section will cope with these questions and phenomena. And then, last, but not least, it will speak candidly about the subjects you're probably hoping you never have to face—career burn-out, job change, coping with job change in a recession, and even getting fired. Certainly, it's probably easier for you in the short term to brush these subjects aside. But increasingly, they're problems more and more workers face. So you'd best be prepared and also have a positive outlook. Then go to the last part of this section: starting a new job.

7

New (or Fast-changing) Career Areas

Blue Collar Jobs: New High-Pay Challenge for Women

Times have changed! In the burly blue collar industrial world, women are doing "men's work," taking home man-sized paychecks, and finding themselves involved in the challenging careers that had shut them out a decade ago.

As the 80's unfold, some industries, faced with an erratic supply of skilled workers in the blue collar ranks and prodded by government EEOC legislation, are hiring women for traditionally male jobs and discovering they perform very well. As for the women, the chance to become electricians, welders, petrochemical workers, and construction workers is freeing them from the economically dead-end jobs in which they were trapped.

At one time, women applying for these kinds of jobs would have been laughed out of the hiring hall. Now, in order to meet EEOC requirements and the urgent need for skilled workers, companies are filling their vacant slots with entry-level women, offering them apprenticeships and on-the-job training. More and more women, both those with low-demand college degrees and those with high school diplomas, are finding jobs as mechanics, bulldozer operators, phone installers, mill workers, die makers, etc. and getting higher pay than they ever thought possible. How can you find out about this kind of opportunity? And is it for you?

Interviews with blue collar workers show that the high pay scale was initially the major attraction for entering this man's world. And why not? The blue collar pay scale, whether one is a bricklayer, truck driver, miner, or welder is much higher than that of bookkeepers and secretaries.

There's one thing you should be aware of—life in the blue collar workplace is quite different from the carpeted office and the temperature-controlled bank or department store.

Blue collar jobs are more physically demanding than white collar jobs. Yet a lot of jobs women currently do for low pay are strenuous too. A waitress in a busy restaurant probably works as hard carrying heavy trays of dishes all day as some highly paid construction workers at building sites. Many blue collar jobs are dirty and one can't spend time worrying about appearance. Hands can get tough, fingernails split, hair tangled by wind. Curls will disappear in humid factories. But there are advantages even to this: you don't have to think about what to wear every morning, and you save money on clothes. Some of the jobs are smelly and some are even hazardous; but once you make the adjustment, there are plusses to be glad about—your great feeling of accomplishment, the challenge of doing a job once considered too tough for a woman, and, of course, the high pay.

But as in all good things, there are any number of requirements to be happy in the blue-collar world. There are still hostilities and harassments that are part of the everyday work life, which will almost demand that you not be ladylike. And you should understand that you could very well be the first to be laid off when cutbacks come. Last hired; first fired. Often, a blue collar job calls for top physical condition, since you may have strenuous working conditions, sometimes outdoors in all kinds of weather. On the other hand, you could find yourself working in highly controlled "clean rooms" assembling tiny temperature-sensitive components for electronic equipment.

Breaking into the blue collar world really calls for a thick skin, stick-to-itiveness, the ability to survive the challenges, the setbacks, the discomfort that every beginner must face. But make no mistake, if you make up your mind, there is no reason why you can't do well in this "man's world." The odds are in your favor right now not only because of EEOC, but because the basic nature of production work and construction work and the various craft fields is changing. The changes are in your favor, that is, there is less sheer muscle power needed; more work is done by advanced machines controlled by, rather than operated by, the workers. A much greater acceptance of women anywhere in the work force also makes it easier now to build a career as a skilled worker.

Careers in Servicing Advanced Office Machines

Photocopy machines. Electronic telephone switchboards. Computer terminals. Typewriters with built-in memories. Word processors. Machines to make copies of letters sent over phone lines.

These are just a few examples of the complex equipment to be found in today's offices. Any or all of them may be the key to a good career for you—but not in using them.

While these new machines make office work easier, they can cause absolute havoc when they break down or don't work right, as you may know. The result is a great need for skilled technicians to repair and service this hi-tech office equipment.

Estimates of the size of this job market vary, with some industry spokesmen saying there may be as many as 100,000 new jobs opening each year. Obviously, in today's economy, this is a career field you should consider seriously.

Some Basic Background on the Jobs   Job titles vary from company to company. Your title might be "technician," "technical service representative," or "associate field engineer." Typical salaries start at least in the mid-teens, depending on experience, says a representative of one major company in the field. Salaries increase rapidly. One organization reports a range after six to eight years' experience of over $20,000 to $25,000, with good upward mobility for supervisory positions.

Large companies also groom their best field service technicians for management responsibility and greater monetary rewards. Many become branch managers and supervise area-wide service. Such managerial jobs can start at over $40,000.

At large companies, a technician with skills and varied interests can follow other career paths as well. You might progress to the point where you are training less experienced personnel; you could study and prepare for promotion to engineering aide or become an engineer, helping to design new equipment.

Large firms are not the only ones hiring. There are many independent service companies in most cities. These firms handle service for small office equipment manufacturers who do not have their own service organizations.

What Does it Take to Start?   Today, as a service technician, you have to combine the hands-on skills of a good mechanic or an electronic troubleshooter with the people-handling skills of a potential manager. Since you'll work independently in customers' offices, a good personality and the ability to take on responsibilities will be important. You also will need to communicate well and promote confidence in your company's products and services.

In addition, obviously, you need real aptitude for handling mechanical and electrical devices and preferably some demonstrated experience. Graduates from two-year technical schools or with the equivalent experience in the military or working for another company are typical of the people sought for such jobs.

Familiarity with specific machines could be helpful, but isn't absolutely necessary, since major manufacturers and service organizations run comprehensive training programs. For example, one company averages 20,000 training sessions a year for over 12,000 technical representatives. The sessions range in length from one day to a week or more. Some major firms also run training programs for the personnel of independent, authorized service companies.

What Are the Jobs Like? A maintenance technician at a laboratory complex in Texas likes making things work and being around research scientists. He had two years of college and some experience in electrical and carpentry work before going to work there, and his job involves repair of research equipment installed by his company.

"I get to see people all over midtown Manhattan," says a service representative for another company. "I like to see their reactions when we get their computer working again. People really appreciate what we do."

Most hiring for service technician jobs is done locally, even if the job is for a national firm. So your best bet is to scan the classified ads in this paper for opportunities, or contact the service offices of office machine manufacturers directly. Addresses and telephone numbers are listed in the Yellow Pages under "Office Furniture and Equipment Repairing and Refinishing," "Typewriters," or "Office Furniture and Equipment Manufacturers and Wholesalers." Computer stores selling to offices are another good source of job leads. If you've got the skills, you're likely to be welcomed with open arms.

What If You Don't Have the Skills? First, find out the kinds of skills that the companies in which you're interested require of people they hire for these technician jobs. Then check locally to determine where you can get solid training that will match these requirements. Usually you can find this at technical or vocational schools within your area, either privately run commercial schools or community-operated systems for adult education. (Be sure to check that the school you select is an accredited one with a good record for placing students in this type of job.) Once you've acquired the basic training, you'll have an excellent chance to get a foot in the door of a very fast-growing and vital new occupation.

Have you considered the advantages of working for a small business instead of a large one? There are certainly enough small businesses in the country to work for: 10.8 million of them according to the Small Business Administration. Forty-three percent of the Gross National Product is generated by these companies and they employ fifty-eight percent of the work force.

Informality and diversity versus security and fringe benefits are some of the contrasts between working for a small business and a large corporation. Of course, there are many options in between the very small, "mom & pop" family operation and the industrial giant, but the job-seeker might want to consider some of the pros and cons of company size when choosing his or her career.

In small businesses, employers want more well-rounded individuals. Since small companies operate on small staffs, they're likely to ask a typist to double as a receptionist or do a little bookkeeping. At a large place, a typist simply puts paper in the machine and types away.

But if there's more potential to learn in a small company, you may be hindered because such a company isn't likely to have the latest model equipment. For example, a small office may not have a computer, a word processor, or even the most advanced electric typewriter.

Balancing this is the greater chance for a middle manager to become a top officer at a smaller company, for a secretary with a flair for promotion to become an advertising manager, and so forth. This kind of rise would take a long time to happen at a larger company with a formal pattern of promotion to be followed. It occurs because each individual in a smaller firm is highly visible. For the same reason, however, you'll have to perform well. A small company can't afford to keep someone who's not contributing.

Another small company hazard is job loss. Such organizations are more likely to lay people off when there is a slack season or business falls off. (Though in recent years this has been equally true of even corporate giants.)

"We were never sure whether we'd get paid the next week or not," said one former employee of a small magazine. "But seeing the smile on a salesman as he came running back with an advertising contract balanced that risk with excitement. I never could have learned as much or had such a good time in a larger place. But, when I felt it was time to make more money, they couldn't afford to give it to me."

The kind of working environment a person wants should be a consideration when looking for a job. Small firms are often less formal. This means that they may have a more relaxed attitude toward dress and less strain in relationships between supervisors and other employees. So if you want to show up in casual clothes and not have to worry about "formal business manners," the right small company may provide you with a comfortable niche.

Many young people looking to their jobs to expand their social contacts prefer to work for a large employer, where there is a bowling team, social club, and opportunities for other after-work activities. People who are reluctant to get to know their coworkers will sometimes look to the large company for just the opposite reason—they prefer the anonymity that often comes with large groups of people.

Fringe benefits are often better at large companies, but not always. It is advisable to compare benefits before making a decision on this basis. Medical plans, life insurance, pension programs, vacations, sick days, and time off for personal business may be more generous with larger companies.

A large employer also is more likely to pay for training courses or college credits that may lead to advancement, and to offer in-house training programs that will increase skills. But a small company offers the opportunity to learn by doing, and you'll have close contact with other skilled employees who are doing jobs you would like to learn.

Small businesses may not make headlines as often as large ones, and you may not even be aware of how many service, trade, and manufacturing businesses there are in your community. But if the idea of working in a small, friendly shop, office, or plant appeals to you, look into the prospects. There is little doubt the risks are higher in going to work for a small business. But often the diverse experience, informal working conditions, and excitement of watching a company grow is worth the risks.

High Demand For Data Processing Professionals

Even in a recession, electronic data processing (EDP) remains one of the hottest career areas. An employment forecast survey shows that while some dips are occurring in other occupations, programmers, analysts, and other EDP specialists are riding through the recession virtually unscathed. Experts also expect that EDP-related occupations, whether trouble-shooting computing machinery or working at the ultra-high level of systems architecture, will be among the most sought-after specialties during the 1980's. For anyone in the process of selecting a career or contemplating a mid-career change, EDP is clearly a field worth serious consideration. Demand and salaries are high and, just as important, so is job satisfaction among EDP professionals.

Why the High Demand?   While the use of EDP has been growing steadily during more than thirty years, new technology offering extensive computing power at low cost and in ever-smaller packages has created new breakthrough markets for computer use in the 1980's. These include the development of computer-based consumer goods, ranging from games and cameras to personal desk-size computers that can cost as little as a television set and may become as widely used.

Another major development is in the "reindustrialization" area: the application of computing power to manufacturing machinery and processes. This area includes not only creating more flexible and versatile machine tools, such as industrial robots, but linking these machines together into whole manufacturing systems.

The offices of America, already affected by the extensive use of computing to handle routine jobs, such as preparing payrolls and providing data storage and retrieval capabilities, are also on the point of being "reindustrialized." One direction in which this is moving is in the provision of personal mini-computers (desk-top size machines) to many people doing specialized jobs, such as marketing and purchasing. At the same time, other advanced office machines, like word processors and facsimile machines, are being mated to computers to develop what is being called "the office of the future."

At the professional and semi-professional level, computers are becoming indispensable aids to engineers, for example, who utilize a development called "computer graphics" to vastly speed up the design of products, equipment, and processes and, at the same time, are reducing the need for drafters and other support people. Computerized medicine is around the corner, and the use of computers to find and analyze legal material is changing the legal profession.

As all of these trends and others, such as the widespread use of computers in the military, gain momentum, the number of people who can design computing hardware (the machines) and software (the programs) will continue to grow. At the same time, the ability to use computers will be the critical skill in the decade ahead; as essential in obtaining a good job as the ability to read and write.

Where to Go for More Information   If you're interested in pursuing a career in data processing, there are several sources you can look into. First, check to see if your company will train you to work with its data processing equipment. Many companies now have DP training programs for employees who want to switch careers. You might want to check with your local community college or high school to see if you can take some courses in computer science. These are expanding rapidly as the opportunities in this field are being recognized by people eager for well-paying, high-demand jobs.

The American Federation of Information Processing Societies, Inc. (1815 North Lynn St., Arlington, VA, 22209), is an umbrella organization of the professional societies serving the U.S. computer industry. They will mail you a brochure about the computer field and, if requested, a calendar of all the trade and professional shows across the country. Many of these shows offer reduced admission rates to students.

Check with your local library for books on the subject, or glance through the "Occupational Outlook Handbook," published by the U.S. Department of Labor. EDP career information is provided in the section, "Office Machines and Computer Occupations." Finally, two of the major trade publications you might want to read are *Computerworld*, a weekly newspaper, and *Datamation*, a monthly magazine.

Personnel: A Challenging Career for the 80's

There is a job category that is growing so fast the government's Bureau of Labor Statistics hasn't caught up with it. It offers good career prospects for the 1980's; the work is interesting, and, if you like the idea of helping people make the most of themselves, it's a field that can bring great personal satisfactions. It is a function basic to all organizations—personnel.

Right now, according to BLS's statistics, there are over 400,000 people working in personnel positions—an increase of 69,000 people in just two years and an employment level that was predicted not for today but for 1985.

Why is the field growing so fast? Because the 1980's have become a decade in which "people power"—as workers—is going to be ever more important. This may sound strange when we see substantial layoffs in different parts of the country and a high unemployment rate. Yet there are many problems in human resources existing right now due to a national lack of trained personnel for new and/or growing fields.

For example, the Bureau of Labor Statistics projects that the need for technicians to service computer equipment is going to triple by 1990. Demand for technical professionals in computing electronics and other "hot" technologies remains very high, despite the recession. A recent study by an industry association says the electronics industry alone could hire nearly 200,000 college grads with electronics or computer science degrees through 1985; but only 70,000 are going to be graduated over the next several years. Personnel people are the ones who must help companies compete for this hard-to-find talent.

They are also the people who, in layoff situations such as are now occurring, arrange "outplacement" assistance to help find new jobs for those displaced due to economic conditions, new technologies, or other reasons.

The major reason that personnel is an expanding field is that corporations are discovering their employees are important not only as scarce talent in many areas, but as sources for increasing productivity, providing new ideas, and working in a new kind of relationship with the company that hired them. This was dramatically expressed by one major company, Motorola, in its advertising in major publications: "Could the individual hold the key to productivity?" the ad asked. The company thinks so and describes its Participative Management Program, where the company gets " the individual worker more involved, more responsible, informed and therefore more productive." The results? "Quality, output, and customer service are way up, costs are down. Our jobs are more satisfying."

It is significant that many companies are changing the name of what was once called "personnel" to the broader and more accurate title of human resources. Further, according to a recent poll by Opinion Research Corporation, sixty-nine percent of the top management people participating and seventy-three percent of the human resources managers expect the importance of this function to increase in the next five years.

How can you get into the action?

First, keep in mind that there is a whole range of activities in which human resources people are involved as managers, experts, or support people. These range from implementing company affirmative action programs to such statistically oriented areas as wage and salary administration. Human resources executives come from all kinds of educational and working backgrounds, including such often overlooked degrees as liberal arts, psychology, and sociology. There are opportunities, too, for non-degreed people who may have such skills as physical training, computer programming (computer use is increasing rapidly in this field), creating audio-visual materials used in training, communications, and so on.

So, second, if you're really motivated to develop a career in human resources, start digging into the literature on the field to learn about the many functions it involves and the many skills in use. The more you know, the better you'll be able to determine where you'd like to fit in and the more you'll convince the interviewer, eventually, that you belong on his or her side of the desk. Check your local library for such trade publications as *Personnel Administration*, *Personnel Journal*, and *Personnel*, to absorb some background.

Once you feel you're ready, there are a number of routes you can take. Perhaps the best way is to talk to people in the human resources department of your own organization. They can tell you about their work and suggest further reading or training. More importantly, these contacts could lead to a chance at the next entry-level opening. In the process, get as much information as you can about schools in your area which offer courses in personnel or provide training for some of the specialized areas that are handled by this department. Since such courses are often taught by people who are currently working in the field, this is another avenue for locating a job. Other routes are your company's job-posting system, people you know outside the company who work in this field, office temporary work agencies (to get experience in a personnel department), and employment agencies which are directly involved with company human resources people.

The leading organization in the field is the American Society for Personnel Administration, 30 Park Drive, Berea, Ohio, 44017. Write them for information on careers in personnel and labor relations. Write, too, to the American Society for Training and Development, 600 Maryland Ave., S.W., Suite 305, Washington, D.C. 20024, for information concerning a career in employee training and development.

Planning Your Career: Never Too Late

When Robert H. graduated from college last June, it was into a job market that had no teaching openings for people with advanced degrees in English. But he was able to use a secondary skill he had acquired in college to land a job. The skill was working with a computer, which he had had to learn in connection with a Ph.D. project on word combinations. Now it helped him win a position writing manuals for use with computers. He soon became fascinated with the whole computer field and started to learn other related skills, including programming. Today, instead of a teaching career, he has planned a promising new career for himself in the rapidly expanding field of data processing.

Robert was lucky to be able to switch his career into a totally different field. But his true story demonstrates what can happen when you specialize in a subject or take a job without considering the long range prospects in the field. You may find yourself, sooner or later, without a job and with no demand for your training or experience. So, ask yourself some questions about your working goals.

Is the market for your job expanding or contracting? Can the skill you are learning be applied to other fields if necessary? Will your present job train you for a higher level one? Is technology likely to make your job outmoded? What are the overall occupational prospects for you in the next ten years?

With the easing of mandatory retirement and the increase of life expectancy, a worker of any age can expect to spend more years working. More than ever, thoughtful career planning can make the difference between a productive, lucrative work life ahead, or being stuck in a low-paying job with obsolete skills. Young workers often assume they have endless time and unlimited opportunities, while older ones may think they have too little time or too few options to make a change. The reality is that no matter where you are—just starting out, mid-career, or close to retirement—it is never too late to develop a career plan. By realistically examining your life experiences, interests, the economy, and the job market, you can determine the direction you want your working life to take in the future and what job possibilities are best to pursue.

Some Planning Basics.   Start out by asking yourself what kinds of work you have done, what you would like to do, how long it will take to achieve this goal, and if you want to invest the time and effort. By sitting down with a pencil and paper and listing all your skills and interests, you may be able to come up with a job you had never thought about before. For instance, if you play the piano, have a good ear, and enjoy craft work, you may be able to become a piano tuner, a skill often in demand. You may be able to combine an untapped knowledge with a present skill to enter a new field.

In choosing a job, you should also consider how technology will affect the field. Technology has created many new jobs, but it has also eliminated many. Supermarkets have virtually replaced small grocery stores, and computers have taken over check-sorting and other mechanical tasks. Try to be sure your skill won't be obsolete in a few years.

Other points to consider: Is the job something that can be done in only one place? Does it have only one funding source? Is it seasonal and dependent on unusual circumstances (*i.e.*, a war economy)? Frank Borman has made a successful transition to president of Eastern Airlines, but most astronauts cannot practice their profession if the government space program is cut back.

Where the Jobs Will Be.   There are over 20,000 job titles. In planning your career you will want to know which of these jobs are expected to be in demand in the coming years. One fast way to find out is to check the *Occupational Outlook Handbook*, a survey by the U.S. Dept. of Labor's Bureau of Labor Statistics. The handbook examines training, educational requirements, and earning potential in over 300 jobs, ranging from bus driving to soil scientist. It also predicts which fields are expected to grow through 1990. Your local public library should have a copy, or check the local office of the Dept. of Labor.

What professions are promising? *Clerical workers* (including secretaries, typists, computer operators, word processors, and sales workers) are the largest and fastest growing group. A whole range of *jobs relating to health care* will expand as the population, particularly elderly people, increases. The increasing population will foster expanded services in finance, insurance, real estate, banking, and credit agencies. *Professional and technical workers* (scientists, engineers, and accountants) are expected to increase. *Craft workers* (tool and die makers, carpenters), *repair workers*, and other jobs requiring vocational training or apprenticeships are in demand.

Which jobs will slow down or decline? Teachers, writers, artists, and pilots will continue to face a tight market. Because of technological advances, the number of agricultural workers will drop. For example, the new hard-skinned tomato will reduce the number of handpickers required. Service work (janitors, household workers, firefighters, security) is very high in demand, but the number of workers available is expected to decline because of the strenuous work, low pay, and negative image connected with this type of occupation.

How to Find Out More.   After all your analyzing and investigating you may want to consult a specialist to help you make the best decisions. High school or college guidance counsellors can be of assistance. If you are already employed, many firms now have "career pathing" programs with scheduled consultations, particularly in the early years of employment, and discussions of career goals as part of performance appraisals. Tuition reimbursement plans can also be included in your total career plan.

Many professional and trade association groups have information for people who want to enter a given field, for example, the American Association of Engineering Societies (AAES) (ask for guidance brochures) or the American Association of Advertising Agencies. To learn names and addresses of organizations in fields of interest to you, check the annual edition of *National Trade and Professional Associations* published by Columbia Books, Inc., Washington, D.C. There are also private "career consultants" available, but fees charged vary widely from several hundred to several thousand dollars. You should comparison shop before signing up with any of these firms.

Women Star in Executive Sales

The natural born salesperson is a woman—not a man. According to David King, president of Careers for Women, a sales training school and placement service, women excel in each of six key areas that determine success in sales—appearance, intelligence, verbal skills, personality, character, and motivation.

Assuming you have these attributes, how do you market them?

Executive sales is one of the most highly paid jobs in the U.S. and often the fastest track to management, according to King, who started his sales and marketing school several years ago to help women learn how they, like men, can earn $40,000 and up a year. It won't happen overnight, but it will happen more quickly for women who seek careers in executive sales or who set up their own businesses. It's in executive sales that the purest buyer–seller relationship exists, he points out. The traditionally low image of the fast-talking salesperson selling products door-to-door has no place at this level. Dispelling the notion of sales as a high-rejection, dishonest field helps many women take the plunge.

Most of the women who come for training already have jobs and are looking for a better way to increase their earnings. One "graduate," for example, spent ten years in banking before making a move. She started out as a secretary and worked her way up to a corporate officer responsible for a branch. Her salary, however, had inched up at a discouraging rate. After six years of selling life insurance, her salary now approaches six figures, and she looks forward to eventually having her own sales office.

The school has offices in New York and Los Angeles and is a three-fold operation: a "school for saleswomen," a placement service, and a consulting service for Fortune 500 companies.

In its "teaching" capacity, the company runs a variety of seminars and workshops throughout the country. Many are free and are conducted on such topics as "How to Select a Career Path in Sales," "How to Take a Sales Interview," and "How to Get a Job." Women learn the kinds of jobs available, how to get them, and the kinds of salaries they can expect. They also learn how to conduct themselves during interviews and how to identify the trade publications that will contain employment ads to meet their job interests. There's a job exchange workshop, one on the psychology of success, and another on "How to Take a Client to Lunch." Free career nights bring back successful grads who describe their career areas, the plusses and drawbacks, and answer questions.

For women who want to start their own businesses, King advises staying away from cosmetics, fashion, travel, and residential real estate since there are many talented women in these fields. The fields to break into and in which to gain a competitive edge are those that are male dominated.

Women more interested in a corporate situation should decide whether they're more comfortable in large or small companies. The best sales areas, King says, are securities, advertising space, industrial supplies, pharmaceuticals, and insurance.

In teaching women how to sell, King shows that everyone is in the "persuasion" business. Social decisions as basic as what restaurant or movie to go to can be translated to the selling situation so that the seller effectively "persuades" the buyer to purchase its product or service.

Before a woman will find herself in that position, however, she first has to get the job. To do so, King recommends checking employment ads daily rather than sending unsolicited résumés. He further advises a woman interviewing for a job to:

- Arrive on time. Lateness usually means you've already lost the job.
- Find out the salary and commission structure. A mark of a successful salesperson is someone concerned about money.

- Ask about the selling situation. Does it call for prearranged appointments with potential buyers? Will you be required to call on clients "cold" (*i.e.*, without an appointment)? What kind of people will you be selling to? Your success depends on being comfortable in the selling situation.
- Find out if travel will be expected. How much travel and to where? What travel expenses will be included?
- Find out the size and quality of the sales force. Is it predominantly male? This may be beneficial as far as assuring good deals regarding commissions, bonuses, and so forth, but you may not be comfortable as the only woman on the staff.

8

Working Smarter

We've spoken a great deal in this book about working smarter. That term includes thinking differently about work and work modes, then acting on those thoughts. Increasingly, as this section indicates, working smarter involves thinking about old assumptions about "correct" means of working and revising them sharply.

For example, "nine to five" at one job, Monday through Friday, isn't a natural law. It's simply just one mode of work in many companies, as they find that employees require many different schedules.

Why? For one thing, economic difficulties have not only increased the numbers of women in the labor force, but also increased the numbers of men *and* women who wish to work more than one job. And the number of people—men and women alike—who have valuable talents but who may not wish to work full time is gradually getting companies accustomed to other than full-time work modes, such as job sharing or permanent part-time status.

The rapid proliferation of computers has made working at home a possibility. And if, in the last section, you heard about women moving into "men's fields," in this section you'll encounter men who have decided to move into what were once considered "women's fields," such as teaching, nursing, and secretarial work, a move which has not only given them personal satisfaction but helped to raise salaries. And you'll meet some resourceful people who are out gaining experience for that first full-time job by working a variety of part-time or temporary positions. A few really entrepreneurial types have even made a "career" out of temporary work.

Being a Permanent Temp

Four years ago, a former Washington school teacher packed up her dog and left her marriage and her home. Her assets? A few dollars in cash, flexibility, and boundless determination. Today she is a permanent temporary, one of the growing number of people who free-lance through life.

She has tackled almost anything from working as a secretary to scrubbing floors. At the beginning of her free-lance career, she worked through employment agencies. Now she's even freed herself of depending on them.

How does she feel about her new career? It's good for people not dependent on security, she says, but requires strong self-discipline.

Perhaps the idea of "temping" without resorting to employment agencies terrifies you. Perhaps you have work—as an artist, writer, or performer—which you need to subsidize by working; but you must keep your schedule flexible. Perhaps you have young children at home part of the time or all of the time. Or maybe you get bored easily and you've had trouble hanging onto a full-time job. And then there are the people right out of school who "don't have any experience" and need to get some. Temporary work—full time—may be your answer.

Consider the case of Thomas G., a writer whose chosen profession makes him a fast typist, an accurate speller, and good in grammar. When he learned word processing last year, he found that his hourly rate for "temping" went up dramatically. Not only that, he now has more jobs to pick and choose among, including higher paying night and week-end shifts. Or Maria L., who is a musician with a lovely voice. When she's not singing or taking classes, she's a receptionist for a variety of businesses, who value her trained speech abilities and stage presence for their ability to project a positive image on visitors. Plus, both Thomas and Maria have paid holidays, including vacations and medical benefits. These are paid for, not by the companies where they've "temped," but by the agency for which they work regularly. Such temp agencies, in order to hold onto valuable "full-time temps" offer them fringe benefits roughly comparable to what they'd receive from other businesses. But, adds Maria, there's another bonus too. Not only does she earn raises for increased skill and length of service with the temporary agency, she also earns the bonus given every temporary worker who successfully completes a given term of service.

How do "full-time temps" organize their schedules and secure work? People who don't use agencies must actively hustle for work on their own; running small classified ads, for example. People who work through temp agencies, on the other hand, might follow the plan Thomas uses.

- He examines his finances and notes that he will need money.
- He determines that his writing can be postponed or slowed while he earns the money by temporary work.
- During the week before he wishes to work, he gets in touch with his temporary agency and informs them. "We'll get back to you later in the week," they tell him; and they do. On the Friday before he starts to work, he learns the name of his temporary employer and the person to whom he'll be reporting.

"You'll have to help out," he comments. "Sometimes they call me on weeks when I hadn't planned to work, and they need someone right then. On maybe three hours' notice. So I go. I can always use the extra money, and besides, these people have been good to me."

Are there any objections to temping full-time? Yes. It's not a career for the insecure. Because there isn't a company hierarchy in which to advance, full-time temps can't expect much in the way of raises or promotions; mostly that's not what they're looking for.

What about the older people or the women who suddenly find, after many years at home, that they need to work? In some cities, there are agencies that specialize in the "mature temp." (Check your phone book's Yellow Pages to see if any are listed.) According to such agencies, companies value such employees' steadiness and respect for work. Some offer brush-up courses to help people returning to the work force burnish their skills.

Are *you* the stuff of which full-time temps are made? Try it. You might like it so well that you'll never go back to a one-company job.

More Opportunities for Men in Nontraditional Jobs

Dave Anderson applied to twenty-three employment agencies before he discovered that his most marketable skill was his ability to type seventy words a minute. That skill landed him a job as secretary in a publishing company. Though people are surprised that he takes dictation and gets coffee for his boss, Dave doesn't mind. He sees his job as an entrée into the business world.

Dave is one of a growing number of men who are taking jobs once held almost exclusively by women. During the past decade, women who wanted the earning power and prestige of jobs held traditionally by men have been working hard to break down the old barriers between "men's work" and "women's work." Now that the stereotypes have begun to erode, men in many parts of the country have begun to feel freer to take "women's jobs."

Male secretaries, phone operators, nurses, and stewards are still the exception to the rule. Nonetheless, many men are attracted to these jobs for a simple reason—demand. "Traditionally male sectors of the economy, such as manufacturing, are declining," says an Institute spokesperson. "Jobs are more readily available in the service sectors of the economy which are expanding and have been traditionally dominated by women."

Certainly that's true of clerical work. The U.S. Bureau of Labor Statistics estimates that one sixth of the total work force is now clerical or secretarial and that the field will grow by an average of 300,000 jobs a year for the next ten years. Many women have become reluctant to take secretarial jobs for fear of being trapped at a typewriter. As a result, some cities are suffering severe secretarial shortages, and men are stepping in to fill the gap.

One New York City temporary agency reports that over a third of the people it places are men. Another national firm awarded a male secretary its employee of the year award. All together, there are an estimated 75,000 male secretaries nationwide with most employed in large cities on the east and west coasts.

Though the idea of a man as a secretary may seem surprising today, it was commonplace a hundred years ago when virtually all secretaries were male. Even in 1910, 75 percent of all secretaries were men, and clerical workers earned twice as much as blue collar workers. In 1980, starting salaries for secretaries in the Federal Government ranged from $9,776 to $15,193. Nationally, annual salaries for secretaries averaged $11,856, according to a survey by the American Management Associations. An executive secretary's salary in the Northeast can go much higher—up to $25,000 or more a year. Word processing skills add more dollars, too.

Many men are attracted to secretarial work because of the working conditions. "I like getting dressed in a suit instead of overalls," says one male secretary. Another remarks, "It may seem more masculine to go out on a telephone truck and string wire, but it's also nice to sit in an air-conditioned office in the summer and have some energy left at the end of the day."

Other men find that secretarial work is a "foot in the door" opportunity to enter business. Younger men who might have taken trainee positions in the past now may learn the business by doing secretarial work for a year or two. Some male secretaries find that their sex earns them special attention and quick promotions from male executives. "I got a lot of encouragement to advance," says one former male secretary.

Nursing is another nontraditional field which is attracting more men. Some male nurses are veterans who worked as medics in Vietnam. Others thought about going to medical school but decided to become nurses because it required less time and money. A registered nurse of either sex must have three years of training and can earn between $14,000 and $20,000 a year depending upon the area of the country and the type of hospital. Finding a job is not a problem since many communities suffer from chronic shortages of nurses especially in rural areas and in big cities.

Some nontraditional jobs appeal to men, not because they are plentiful, but because they allow men to develop aspects of themselves which are not encouraged in traditional jobs. For example, there are approximately 70,000 new jobs for kindergarten and elementary school teachers each year. Ninety-nine thousand people apply for those jobs, and the percentage of men is increasing. "That's because the women's movement made men look hard at their own lives," says the male director of a day-care center. "Many weren't happy with the stereotyped masculine images that are forced upon us. Teaching young children allows men to develop as nurturing people."

Of course, taking on nontraditional jobs isn't always easy. For one thing, men in "women's jobs" often find that people are unable to accept them for what they are. "Nursing has maternal overtones," complains one male nurse. "People think I'm an orderly or a doctor but they can't accept me as a nurse." Other men find that they are the butt of jokes or insinuations that they are homosexuals.

In general, however, men who take nontraditional jobs face the same occupational problems as women. Bosses ask male secretaries to get coffee and run personal errands; customers are rude to male telephone operators; and passengers make passes at male flight attendants. In some cases, they must also contend with the low salaries which have traditionally been attached to "women's jobs." That, however, may be changing because, as one male nurse put it, "Guys get together and organize and are willing to fight for more."

Whether that's true or not, one thing is certain: The lines between "men's work" and "women's work" are getting fuzzier every day.

Moonlight Madness

Have you ever thought of taking a second job? Most of the time one job is enough to keep you busy and then some. Then comes the first of the month, and your salary won't stretch to cover all the bills. Even with a spouse or roommate to share expenses, most people are finding it harder to make ends meet. If you had *two* paychecks, things would look a lot brighter.

In this chancey economy it's easy to understand why people feel compelled to take second jobs. But while "moonlighting" may sound romantic and help pay those bills, working more than eight hours a day can be exhausting.

The Bureau of Labor Statistics says more than four million people are now engaged in second jobs. Some forty percent of them do it for extra income to meet regular expenses; ten percent are paying off debts; 20 percent are saving for education and future projects. Finally, 30 percent have nonfinancial motives, such as enjoying the work. This group includes Ben, a foreign language teacher who supplements his salary by playing the organ for church services, concerts, and other events. Harriet, a stock clerk gets up at 4 A.M. daily to work on her novel. While different than a regular job, writing is serious business for her. She hopes the published book will provide retirement income, along with, hopefully, an inheritance for her children.

Barbara is a secretary who has held a second job in the accounting department of a hotel for three years. The hardest part is the rigid schedule which leaves her no free time between 6 A.M. when she leaves home until sometime after 9 P.M. when she returns. Eating out twice a day cuts into her income, but Barbara is proud of the three-bedroom townhouse she has bought and furnished.

If you've been considering a second job, or a money-making home business, here are some things to think about:

1. *Consider all your options first.* Since you're already working, you can afford to choose your second job more carefully. What occupations are you qualified for which will best fit in with your current work and your goals?

2. *Analyze the financial aspect.* If the second job increases expenses for food (eating out is costly), travel, clothing (uniforms, for example), dues, child care, and other costs, you may actually spend more than you make by moonlighting.

3. *Figure the cost in time.* Take a serious look at your present schedule, including all commitments. How would you fit them around a second job? What time-related sacrifices would two jobs demand? Can spouse, in-law, or older children assume more responsibilities at home?

4. *What about moonlighting for your full-time employer?* Is it possible you could work additional hours (for additional pay) reducing travel cost and time spent commuting from place to place, not to mention the hassle of adjusting to new surroundings, supervisors, coworkers, and responsibilities?

5. *Consider a change of pace from your usual routine.* Why not opt for a change of pace, in terms of duties, environment, and exposure to

the public? If you're isolated in a lab or office all day, you might enjoy the social stimulation of working as a restaurant host or hostess or hotel desk clerk, for example.

6. *Would a home business be a preferable alternative?* If you have a flair for creating useful products and selling them, the opportunities are endless. Many women market their own needlework designs. The family can work together in a small mail-order business. A part-time enterprise allows you to adjust your schedule and work load to meet other demands, keep an eye on your children, and otherwise fit the job to your needs.

7. *Work a trial period.* If you've never tried a second job before, a temporary position allows you to evaluate the situation. You might discover, for example, that you can tolerate three additional hours, but not on your feet.

8. *Consider distances to be traveled.* With the cost of cars, fuel, and public transporation at an all-time high, a job that's close to home is practical, even if it pays somewhat less. If you must increase your work load, try to avoid increasing your travel time, too.

9. *Consider the benefits available through a second job.* Perhaps you can plan them to complement those related to your full-time position. Additional life insurance, health care, and profit-sharing opportunities may justify your extra effort.

10. *Consider your individual stamina, personality, feelings, and needs.* A second job that suits you and meets your needs will be less tiring. Maybe there's something important you'd like to do with your life. Frustrated school teachers find an outlet in teaching adult education programs. Actors, musicians, and other performers can't always find full-time employment in their fields, but part-time work may be plentiful. If you've always wanted to work with children, the handicapped, or the elderly but felt the pay was too low to do it full time, a part-time position allows you to reap the rich rewards of service to others.

For many people, moonlighting is a satisfying experience; yet for others it's not worth the effort. With a bit of planning, it can be the opportunity of a lifetime for you.

Job Sharing: Pairing Up to Pare Down Work Time

Some uncommon people, like astronomers, parole officers, and career counselors, are working in an uncommon way. They're dividing themselves in half. Further, they are doing it so successfully that many employers are beginning to take notice. Which means a new way to work may be opening up for many of us. It's called job sharing, a flexible work arrangement that is catching on as an alternative to the forty-hour week.

Job sharers form a partnership, splitting the time spent on the job while sharing the salary, responsibilities, and fringe benefits. People who are attracted to the idea of job sharing usually feel that their time is more important than money. And the days they gain are used to devote to their families, to building a career, going to graduate school, or even starting their own business. Or they may just relax and enjoy their reprieve from a hectic schedule.

Many job sharing teams are women, but not all. Some nineteen percent are male–female teams (married couples are included) and nine percent are two-man teams. Women with small children, senior citizens, and free-lancers find job sharing particularly appealing. Right now, job sharers at a New York life insurance company have a week-on, week-off arrangement. Robert Gilman, an astrophysicist and professor of astronomy, shares his job, too. The other half of the time he spends on fascinating personal projects like building his own solar home. Two women in Portland, Oregon, each work two-and-a-half days a week, the half being the Wednesday they meet to discuss their job. In Wisconsin, two parole officers, a man and a woman, worked a half year each at one full-time job. They were part of "Project JOIN," a demonstration to test job sharing and flexible time arrangements.

Is Job Sharing for You?   It might be a way in which you can combine the benefits of a steady, interesting job with having large blocks of time to do other work that's important to you. For example, if you'd like to build a career in another field, you can invest the time it takes minus some of the financial risks. If you're a free-lancer, having a shared job can give you roots and a steady income plus the chance to handle your own business. Or it can give you more time to devote to your family.

Job sharing can open up new avenues for older employees, too. They may share the job with another younger person while phasing out of their working life. The partner, meanwhile, is gaining valuable experience. Or two senior people can split a demanding job, augment retirement income, and maintain ties with the company.

What about drawbacks? Job sharing cannot give you all the benefits of a full-time job. Your paycheck, for one thing, is cut in half. However, your free-lance or second career work may make up for it. Generally, you won't receive the usual benefits. Or if these are provided, they will not be as extensive as a full-time employee receives. Then, too, when it comes to advancement, people are seldom promoted as a pair. The costs of working are the same as on a full-time job in some ways, such as a suitable wardrobe. But some costs, such as transportation, could be cut in half if you work alternate weeks or half weeks. For those involved, however, the time to pursue other interests more than compensates.

Why Some Companies Encourage Job Sharing.   Companies who have tried job sharing teams are discovering some unforeseen advantages. An expert at a New York consulting firm that specializes in job sharing and work-time alternative programs explains that job sharing benefits a company by allowing it to retain valuable employees. Take the example of one woman who wanted to spend time with her new baby. She convinced her employer that she could share her job with a capable friend, whose background complemented her own. This gave the employer a "super employee" with a wide range of skills. Since the women covered for each other when one was ill or on vacation, the employer had no problems with absenteeism.

Another problem alleviated by job sharing is turnover. Partners are reported to be highly committed to their job and take pride in the success of the team. The communication and cooperation between the people sharing the job also promotes job satisfaction.

According to a General Mills study, "Families at Work; Strengths and Strains," job sharing is expected to grow. Although only twelve percent of the companies polled have actually tried job sharing in the past five years, their experiences are paving the way for more partnerships.

How Do You Get into Job Sharing?   Some partners jump right in and answer help wanted ads and propose they share the job advertised. If their combined skills cover the job description and offer the benefits of job sharing to the employer, the partners are called in for an interview. Others have applied for jobs individually and then propose job sharing at the interview.

Proposals from employees sometimes encourage a manager to restructure a job for sharing. The change comes from within the organization itself and can be effected at all levels, including professionals. Some who have shared their jobs include: an anesthesiologist, career counselor, city planner, engineer, librarian, museum curator, pediatric intern, program developer, project director, publisher, social worker, and science/feature writer.

Working at Home

Home work used to be something children did after school. But today, it's a way of life for millions of Americans. Three and a half percent of all employed people now work at home. And some experts predict that fifteen percent of us will be working at home by 1990.

Home work has obvious appeal for women who want to work and be available to their children. Men, however, are also choosing to work at home because it gives them more independence and freedom from pressure. Some people find that they can concentrate better at home so they can be more productive. And others are glad to save time and energy by giving up the daily commute.

Basically, two groups of people work at home. First, there are professional people and entrepreneurs who work for themselves. Regional sales reps, accountants, counselors, writers, and other professionals can work just fine in a spare room equipped with a desk, phone, and filing cabinet. Entrepreneurs, starting on a shoestring, often save money by working out of their homes. People have set up beauty parlors in refurbished garages, craft classes in the cellar, and day-care centers in the playroom. Other entrepreneurs, such as chimney sweeps and party planners, use their homes as a base of operations.

Of course, not everyone wants the pressure of working for themselves. Yet now, thanks to computers, people who work for large companies are also working at home. In such cases, the company installs a computer or word processing terminal in the employee's home. The employee can do jobs such as transcribing dictation, keypunching information, or even computer programming on the terminal. When the work is finished, the employee uses the telephone to connect the home terminal to the company's central computer.

Most of the companies that have tried home work like it because they don't have to expand their offices. Also, they can recruit workers who might not otherwise be willing to work. Some people complain, however, that home work makes it impossible for the government to enforce worker protection laws governing overtime, minimum wages, and child labor. In some industries, home work is actually illegal. The garment industry, for example, used to employ people to do "piecework" in their homes. The employee was paid by the number of ski caps knitted or blouses made. Today, the cost of commuting is so high that people in rural areas would like to do piecework at home and the laws prohibiting it are under attack.

What Are the Advantages to You?   Saving money is one of the biggest reasons for working at home. If you don't leave the house, you don't have to pay for bus fare or gasoline. In addition, you can often economize on clothes, since you can wear what you please, and on lunches, since you can prepare your own food at home.

Another big plus is flexibility. Many people who work at home can keep their own hours, sleeping in one day if they wish and working late on another. The flexibility also makes it easier to combine other activities with working. Parents can be home when the children get home from school; a student can take daytime classes and so on.

Finally, home work is the only way in which some people can be employed. Handicapped people, for example, often cannot go to an office, so some companies are training them to use computer terminals in their homes. Similarly, people with young children or aged parents may not be able to leave them at home alone. Home work allows these people to earn extra money without leaving the house.

Some Drawbacks.   Yet, despite the advantages, home work isn't for everybody. Those who do it report that home work requires special discipline. There's no boss telling you what to do and when to do it. Instead, most home workers have to get themselves motivated in the morning and decide when they've done "enough" to quit. As one home worker says, "The hardest part is putting yourself on a schedule."

Distractions are another big problem you may encounter. People who work at home notice that the lawn needs to be cut and the living room needs to be vacuumed. Some find that it's hard to concentrate on their work when the television is on in the next room. Others find that neighbors assume that anyone who's home during the day should be free for coffee and conversation. "People don't take you seriously," says one home worker, "you have to be very firm about the fact that you're working."

Those who are disciplined enough to work at home still face a big problem—loneliness. "In an office," says one home worker, "you talk to people on coffee breaks and lunch breaks, and there's always a sense of having people around you." Home workers, on the other hand, must spend long stretches of time alone. Some people enjoy it, and others find themselves waiting by the door to talk to the postman.

Another factor to consider is that working at home takes you out of the business or professional mainstream. Professional isolation is a problem for people working at home, warns one expert. Because of this, it's hard for them to find out if their pay rates are in line, or how other workers have improved procedures, or even if their problems are shared. As a result, home workers often must make a special effort to read publications, attend conferences, and form networks with other people in the same field.

As an entrepreneur who works at home, you face all the usual anxieties associated with running your own business. At the outset, there may be little income until the business becomes established. In addition, people who work for themselves must play many roles ranging from bookkeeper to publicity agent.

Finally, a thought that seldom occurs when considering this working mode: Working at home may mean that you have nowhere to go to escape from the pressures of the job.

How do you learn whether you have what it takes to work at home? Necessity is the best motivator. Success manages to come to those who find the need to generate income.

Finding a Part-time Job

If you're thinking of finding a part-time job, you're right in the swing of a major new trend in the American economy. Since 1963, the numbers of people working part-time in the U.S. have steadily increased to the point that they now represent about fifteen percent of the total work force.

Companies like the idea. "Part-Time Work Force is Highly Productive," ran the headline in a recent issue of a business journal. "They're productive and plentiful and many companies couldn't get along without them. What's more, they're growing faster than any other segment of the work force," said the opening paragraph.

How do you get into the act?

First: Select a Goal.   Before diving into the part-time work pool, do some thinking. You should, in fact, develop a personal plan that outlines your objectives: what you want to get out of your investment in a part-time position, as well as what you have to offer to an employer.

For instance, is your major goal making money? If so, then this will condition the type of work you should aim at; you should determine where the pay is best for the talents you have. Perhaps, instead, you're thinking that part-time experience may help you obtain the kind of full-time work that appeals strongly to you. Or you may be most concerned with doing work that gives you personal satisfaction. Usually, our motivations are a combination of the three: money, career advancement, and personal achievement. You have to decide what the balance is in your own particular case.

Evaluate Your Marketability.   With your goal in mind, realistically appraise your skills and experience. Can you work with figures, type, file, take shorthand? paint rooms or pictures? sell products, services, or ideas? Until people sit down and make an inventory of them—on paper—they aren't really aware of the range of skills they have to offer. Take driving a car for example; most of us can do it, yet wouldn't think of it as a skill we could sell. Yet driving a taxi cab or a school bus is one of the most common of part-time jobs. So work up your personal list, and ask people who know you to help, they'll be more aware of some of your abilities than you are.

Now, see how these skills match with the goals you've set. Do the key skills need some brushing up, or do you need to acquire additional skills? If you're going back to office work after years of absence, or if you'd like a part-time newspaper job to help launch a writing career, you may need to take brush-up courses before trying for a job. Local community colleges, "Ys," and adult education programs are low cost ways to do this. Or you may want to sign up with a commercial school that will prepare you for office work, TV repair service, or whatever.

But remember, it's not just skills that are the key to job finding. There are certain qualities and personality traits that are useful in the job market. The employment director of a major securities firm told me, "Selling experience is useful in our field, but what we really look for is the personality of the individual: the successful people, whatever their experience, are those who are confident and aggressive—those who can make fifty calls a day, get turned down, yet not be turned off." The same basic concept applies to part-time jobs. The ability to maintain enthusiasm and knock on a lot of doors is a key to successful door-to-door sales; a strong sense of responsibility and a keen sense of observation may qualify you as a security guard.

Use Your Imagination.   Other possible sources of marketable skills are your interests, hobbies, or volunteer work. Your school baby-sitting experiences might suggest working in a day-care center. The sewing you do at home might qualify you for part-time work in a fabric store or in demonstrating sewing machines. Volunteer fund raising for your local charitable organizations isn't too far removed from sales work. And so on.

One way to prod your imagination is to look over the listings in the Yellow Pages of your telephone book and to carefully read the employment advertising in your newspaper. As you read, ask yourself what you could be doing for these companies? If good muscles are one of your assets, maybe a moving and storage company can make use of them. Department stores and factories are open longer hours and often rely on part-time people. Look into the possibilities with organizations that operate on tight budgets—a welfare agency or museum, for example— since these often utilize part-time people by necessity. Check organizations that have heavy loads during certain times of the week— resorts with heavy week-end traffic, publishers who must get their products out on Thursday and Friday for Sunday distribution, businesses that augment staff during holidays, and so on.

"Temps" and Job-splitting.   The temporary help agencies are an obvious place to go for part-time work, particularly if you have clerical and office skills. Keep in mind, too, that some of these agencies offer other than office jobs in that they cover the blue collar field.

Job-splitting, in which two people fill an eight-hour job, each handling four hours' worth, is an idea that is gaining recognition. You and a friend with similar abilities might present themselves as a team for such employment. Check the other section in this book (and the references at the back) on job-sharing for more information.

Applying for a part-time job requires the same effort as obtaining a full-time job: punctuality, neatness, and advance preparation. It helps, however, to be flexible in arranging time schedules.

The foremost question in an employer's mind is, "What can this applicant do for me as a part-time employee?" If you can convince him or her that you will work hard to advance the company's interests, not just your own, you'll soon be on the payroll. Good luck.

Does Permanent Part-time Pay?

"Phased retirement," "mothers' hours," "job-sharing," "working my way through college"—what do all these phrases have in common? They all refer to people who put in less than thirty-five hours a week on a particular job. Unlike temporary workers who regularly move from one office to another or free-lancers who solicit assignments to do on their own time, part-timers are permanently on a company's payroll. The main difference between part-timers and full-time staff is the number of hours they work.

Over twenty million people are classified as part-time workers. They are the fastest growing segment of the American labor force. Some two-thirds of this group are women, and one-fourth are teen-agers. Statistics also show that twenty percent of all unemployed workers are actively seeking part-time jobs as compared with five percent in 1950.

There are many reasons why part-time work has become increasingly popular with both employers and workers. Let's take a closer look at this kind of work to see if it will meet your employment needs.

Who Are They?   Mary J., a high school senior, works two evenings and Saturdays as a salesgirl in a department store. She says, "I enjoy meeting people. This job gives me extra cash, and I can use my store discount to buy clothes and other things."

John G. is paying his college tuition by working on the evening shift at the local branch of a fast-food chain.

Laurie S. works in a nearby electronics plant from 9 a.m. to 2:30 p.m. and then leaves to pick up her children after school. This schedule is very popular with suburban women and is known as "mothers' hours."

Walter P. is a retired elevator operator who resumes his old job on weekends when younger workers prefer to take off.

Marshall S., a former bank official who quit his job to take up farming, conducts corporate financial interviews for a research firm two days a week.

Lenny G., an aspiring actor, sells insurance half the week and goes to auditions the rest of the time.

These are just some examples of the many part-time people woven into the fabric of the work force. Their motives vary: Some need to supplement their spouses' incomes so they can improve their standard of living. Others are pursuing an education or making a career change and need a financial anchor until they reach their goal. A few want more leisure time and are willing to take a cut in income. Still others are not pressed for cash, but want the stimulation of a formal work situation. If any of these aims apply to you, permanent part-time work is worth considering.

How Are They Doing?   Employers are generally happy to have you on the payroll. The consensus is that part-timers are highly satisfactory employees who appreciate the opportunity to make their own hours. In fact, a recent U.S. Labor Dept. survey of sixty-eight major corporations found that there is greater loyalty and enthusiasm and less absenteeism among part-time workers. Companies also report that hiring permanent, part-time people puts less strain on total budgets, because costly overtime payments to regular staff and seasonal hirings and firings can be avoided. Part-timers also are less likely to become bored with work that is repetitious or tired with work that is physically strenuous because they are doing it for fewer hours than full-time people. This is another advantage for you, as well as for the employer.

Although most employers hire part-timers with the idea they will remain on that basis, there are many instances where talented people have been discovered and invited to join full-time. One high school student, Mary L., who worked part-time in a trendy New York department store, was asked to join a training program for buyers after she graduated. The store was a national pace setter, and competition for such spots was keen, but the flair she exhibited in her part-time work gave her an edge over outside candidates.

The Perils of Part-Time.   Part-time work has its drawbacks. Until recently part-time workers have received salaries very close to the minimum wage, and almost no benefits. So, the convenience of the hours was offset by the low income. (It is hard to manage if part-time work is your sole means of support.) Now, however, more than half of all firms in the Labor Department study offer part-timers pro-rated benefits, including sick leave, vacations, and some type of life/medical/retirement insurance. Indications are that this trend will spread in the next few years, especially since experts predict the use of part-timers will increase throughout the economy. In choosing a part-time job, be sure to check the benefits situation.

Another pitfall to avoid is taking jobs to swell the family paycheck, then spending as much as or more than you are bringing in. Since you'll spend less time at home, you'll tend to pay more for services, for fast-foods, cleaning, eating out, and a better wardrobe. This factor needs to be considered if extra money is your reason for taking a part-time job.

Where the Part-time Work Is.   Two areas of the economy that are growing rapidly are retailing and service industries.

This means that stores, repair shops, restaurants, supermarkets, hospitals, hotels, factories, banks, and other institutions not restricted to standard working hours are the best targets for you. MacDonald's, the fast-food chain, estimates that ninety percent of its workers work part-time. So do half of Howard Johnson's workers. Control Data's bindery in Selby, Massachusetts, operates completely with part-time personnel. The morning shift consists of working mothers, and the afternoon shift is made up largely of students. (Absenteeism at the plant, incidentally, runs about three percent compared with eight percent for the corporation overall.) Select a general area that interests you, such as health care, then contact organizations near you and ask. You may be welcomed with open arms.

9

Moving On

In a time of extensive change in the nature of work, coupled with economic fluctuations and worry about employment, anxiety, restlessness, and stress are common. After all, this talk about "career enhancement" is fine assuming you have a career to enhance, or even a full-time position to go to in the morning. But when your job seems to be in jeopardy, normal dissatisfactions, which might have led you to seek a new job, can build up into a feeling of being trapped, of having to hang on at all costs. And such feelings can easily escalate into stress and that new buzz word, burn-out.

However, there is hope. Our attitudes about job change, layoffs, and on-the-job problems are changing. Certainly, no one's going to advise you to run off recklessly, or to job-hop. Yet there's no reason for you to feel either trapped by a job or devastated without one.

As we've said before, what this book is about is working smarter. Smart workers face topics that other people are afraid to cope with: job change, the recession, burn-out, and layoffs. After all, ultimately they're going to lead to a brighter prospect: starting a good new job.

Changing Jobs—Look Deep Before You Leap

How does it happen? You find out six months after moving into a new job that the advantages you thought existed have melted away; that you are stuck in a job from which there is no movement but out, that is to start all over again at job finding; that the company is shaky financially, is readying a move to another part of the country, is involved in a merger, or is striking out in a new direction for which your experience does not qualify you.

Obviously, the time to find out about these hazards is *before* you change jobs. Anyone who has ever had a job interview has experienced the probing questions that interviewers ask to find out about *you*. But remarkably few people ever ask more than general, superficial questions about the company; and even these tend to accept what the company person says about it.

Let's look at some questions you should be asking before accepting a new job as well as some possible sources for answers. Here's a checklist of points that will help you build a profile of the company (and could well make a difference in the pattern of your future success or failure on a new job).

- About the company itself: How long has it been in business? Who are its executives? Is it financially stable? What kind of reputation does it have as an employer?

- What are the company products or services? Is the demand for them growing or diminishing? Sometimes a product or service or a whole industry is in a changing or declining market, with a replacement or a new technique already on the horizon. (Look at the quick growth of word processing or the personal computer.)

- Do the company products face competition from foreign manufacturers that would affect its profits in the U.S.? Plant closings throughout the country underline the importance of this fact.

- Where does the company stand in the industry vis-à-vis its competition? Is it an old prestigious firm or a zesty newcomer? Is it noted for innovation?

- How does it stand on affirmative action? If you're a minority or a woman, this point could shape your future. Even with today's emphasis on the working woman, there are still firms who do not have an active advancement policy for women employees. A woman hired as a secretary in such a company will probably stay a secretary, no matter how bright or how hard she tries. Carol J. is an example. As assistant in Sales, she talked to clients, handled their orders, and sold the product in the showroom. When it came time for the company's national sales meetings, Carol stayed home (for ten years) until a competitor realized she was a prize sales person and hired her away.

- What does the company offer as benefits? Some companies have more than just basic health insurance; they have stock-buying plans, credit unions, retirement benefits, internal training programs, and tuition for further study. (This could be a big factor in advancement.)

- How does company compensation compare with other firms in the field? What are its policies on raises, overtime, bonuses?

- What is the working environment? Having a pleasant or well-equipped place to work says a lot about the company's regard for its employees, contributes to daily performance, a feeling of well being, and in some cases your health.

How You Can Find Out What You Need to Know.   Unfortunately, the easy sources that come to mind won't help. The company interviewer won't reveal company skeletons, and employment agencies are dedicated to filling the job. But there are other—if less easy—sources open to you:

1.   *People who know the company.* These include friends or relatives who have worked there or who know people who have. Maybe they can arrange an introduction to an employee—friend. Social contacts are a good source, too. Fellow club members or members of your church, may work at the company or know someone who does. However, you have to actively seek out such people and have clear ideas on what to ask them.

2.   *Company personnel.* You can meet them at career seminars or open houses. (Watch your newspaper for announcements.) There are company reps at conventions and trade shows that you may meet and talk with. Sometimes, too, companies are involved in community events, which gives you a chance to meet employees informally. Don't however, depend on a single contact; try to get a cross section of opinion.

3.   *Printed material by the company*—the annual report, the company house organ, product brochures, information booklets. Many companies also publish brochures on their history and accomplishments.

4.   *Readers' Guide* and other reference sources at the library. Seek out articles that have appeared about the company in business, trade, and professional journals, as well as in national magazines.

5.   *Your local paper.* Keep an eye on the business pages for current news.

6.   If you have access to a *broker*, get his or her evaluation.

7.   *Business reference sources*, such as Standard & Poor's and Dun & Bradstreet, give useful thumbnail summaries.

8.   Study *company ads* in the newspapers, professional magazines in their field, and national ads, and on TV.

Before you finish, you may feel like an investigative reporter. But the time will be well spent if it means you move into the right job at the right time.

People are less likely to change jobs or switch their careers during shaky economic times when the unemployment rate is, or has been, high; companies in many industries have initiated temporary layoffs or permanent shutdowns; unemployment has hit record levels; and the market for a wide variety of jobs is getting tighter. If you're picking such a time to be dissatisfied, most people would advise you to stick it out. And so you try to. But what do you do if you feel that you've absolutely got to make a change?

As a key to analyzing your situation, here's how university students studying to be career counsellors arrived at solutions for some people.

Consider Barbara P.'s situation. She said she hated her job, and her increasing absenteeism record substantiated this contention. She was arriving at her office late, several days a week. As her typing got sloppier, her lunch hours got longer. "I'm not happy in the office," she said, "but I can't quit. We need my paycheck more than ever." What should she do? Should she seek other employment?

The counselling class concluded that if Barbara were at all interested in moving to a different company, her work record—performance, attendance, attitude—would have reflected her desire to obtain good future references. If she were looking for another job, she would have already moved in that direction. She wanted to be fired, they unanimously concluded.

The professor confirmed that Barbara was hoping to be fired. Through her career awareness counsellor, she realized that she had been pushed by her husband to enter the job market before she was ready. "Did she get fired?" some students asked. No, she finally quit because of her psychological problems. After personal and career counselling, *she* decided that she was ready to reenter the employment world on a part-time basis, and, the class was told, she's now happily employed as a "temp," working two or three days each week.

Michael B. doesn't know what to do. He's been with his firm for three years as an assistant in the marketing department of a large company. Last year he was passed over for a promotion. "I thought it was time to change, but I wasn't prepared to take the gamble. My wife and I are saving to buy a luxury condominium," Michael said. Since he lost the promotion, he says he doesn't have the enthusiasm he originally brought to the job. Because of his change in attitude, the job has become daily drudgery for him.

The future career counsellors suggested that Michael check the price of the type of condominium he and his wife want to buy. He'll find, they assumed, that the price of the condominium keeps increasing. He's already lost a year by paying rent instead of a mortgage. More important, he has lost a year in furthering his career. It doesn't pay, they concluded, for Mike to stay in a rut.

The expert agreed with the consensus of his class. Here were the burgeoning symptoms of a career rut. Michael was advised to make a plan of action. He drew up a plan which reflected his concern for security as he placed the least risky alternatives at the top.

First, he decided to speak to his supervisor about short-term opportunities for advancement. If his supervisor failed to make any hopeful assurances, he would look into a transfer to a related department. He would also investigate company opportunities which meant relocation. His wife was willing to move to another part of the country provided the company had an equitable relocation program and would provide her with job placement services. His final alternative was to begin an active search for a new job.

Michael spoke to his supervisor who told him that within a year he could expect a raise and a promotion. Like a recharged battery, Michael put new energy into his job and gained new self-esteem. A few weeks later, his wife noticed an advertisement for a job that appeared to present better opportunities. He applied, interviewed, and was made an offer. Michael returned to his supervisor and said that unless the company was willing to match the offer now, he was giving two weeks' notice. The company didn't come through, and Michael resigned to take the other position. He worries sometimes about that "last hired, first fired" adage, but he says it's better than constant daily drudgery on a job he had outgrown.

John Z. has been working with a private placement agency for nine months. He wants to leave teaching "to work in the real world and make some bucks. I like teaching but the money is awful," he told the employment interviewer. John has gone to several interviews and received a few offers. One pays nearly twice his present salary, but he hasn't accepted. Should John really begin a new career in the business world?

Answers for John are not so easy. The students in the career counselling program were divided. One group maintained John had not demonstrated the initiative to leave teaching. Why did he interview for jobs he really doesn't want, some wondered? If he really wants to make more money, why doesn't he grab the high-paying job? He's only going through the motions.

John is happy in the classroom and secure with his employment, the other group concluded. But money is a primary motivation, too. All he needs is the confidence to give the business community a try. He can always go back to teaching. John did just this. He took a year's leave of absence to protect himself in case his new career didn't work out. Was he happy in his new slot? No, he returned to the classroom the next semester. He's now considering moonlighting in business to supplement his teaching salary.

Should you take the risk of leaving a job in a negative climate? Determine, first, if it's the job that's got you down, or something else that is bothering you. Don't make a hasty move. Decide what you want from the job—money, satisfaction, challenge, or opportunity. Rank them in order of preference. Devise a plan to add those qualities now lacking in your present employment. For example, you may be able to increase your income through overtime, or you can add challenge to the job by volunteering for a special assignment or learning to operate some new equipment. While working to make your present job more rewarding, investigate other career opportunities. By the time that first offer comes, says the professor of career couselling, you'll have determined whether or not you are really sick of your job.

Career Burn-Out: What to Do When You've Had Enough

One morning Alice L. woke up with a sinking feeling, realizing the last thing she wanted to do was go to her job at a government social service agency in Philadelphia.

"I was overwhelmed by all the details of the job and felt I was drowning in them," she said. "I thought that even if I could master the logistics, I couldn't begin to help the people I was dealing with. I had no real input into the system, which was very regimented. I felt I was just one small, helpless person in a messy world."

Alice was suffering from a classic case of career burn-out. In a constant state of depression, she was unable to concentrate, moody, and tearful at home, and angry and hostile at work to both coworkers and clients. She sought emotional comfort in eating binges and shopping trips.

Career burn-out is what workers get when they can no longer enjoy or cope with their jobs. Not all cases of career burn-out are triggered by the same factors. Nor do they always manifest the same symptoms. Career burn-out can be attributable to workaholism, failure to delegate authority, lack of tolerance for the viewpoints of others, or negative aspects of the job environment itself.

Many people who suffer from career burn-out are often in high pressure jobs with constant strain or much personal contact, such as air traffic controlling, waitressing, and health care work.

Besides the fact that quitting her job wouldn't have gotten to the root of the problem, Alice couldn't afford to because of astronomical monthly house payments. She had left her first love, retailing, because of the long hours and low pay, to opt for the financial security of civil service.

At the suggestion of a supervisor to whom she turned for help, Alice went to a counselling service for government employees. A psychologist there and her own medical doctor together devised a regimen of cognitive therapy for thirteen weeks and antidepressant medication to combat her depression.

Alice, who has continued to take the medication in the eight months since she first sought help, is feeling much better. She credits her psychologist and doctor for the improvement and says she has also been helped by taking a part-time, after-hours job as a product representative.

"I used to think of myself as the world's troubleshooter. I now realize I'm not responsible for the city of Philadelphia, the state of Pennsylvania, or even the world," Alice, a former Peace Corps volunteer says, smiling.

A student intern, who is working on his master's degree in social work at the John F. Kennedy Child Development Center at the University of Denver, has helped to do a comprehensive survey of the literature on burn-out. The results: The discovery that burn-out isn't a sudden thing or the result of any one cause. Burn-out tends to sneak up on people.

And its effects on individuals can include feeling fatigued, becoming cynical, spending more time than is needed on paper work to avoid dealing with people, watching television excessively at home, and escaping with drugs and alcohol.

Since burn-out is currently a very fashionable term, do be careful that you don't use it to conceal other work problems. Career burn-out isn't exhaustion; it occurs when the actual content of the job no longer satisfies, according to Dr. Margaret Baker of the Center for the Study of Adult Development. She added that career burn-out should not be confused with a more general need to reevaluate one's life in terms of personal matters like marriage and total life direction.

Problems that can masquerade as burn-out but don't fit her strict definition, she said, include working in a physically or emotionally uncomfortable work environment, becoming a scapegoat for a dissatisfied supervisor, developing a dislike for coworkers, or letting personal problems affect the job.

What to do if you're burned out? Sometimes quitting is the only solution—and this adds to the anxiety that the burn-out victim is already feeling. As awful as the job may have become, what will happen to bills, to house payments, to all those hundreds of expenses without it. But Dr. Baker notes that people often unnecessarily regard the career choices of their late twenties or even later years as irrevocable.

For a Colorado school teacher who suffered from burn-out for the last three years of her five years of teaching, quitting was a happy solution.

Dana M. recalls that her frustrations with the educational system grew as her career progressed. Its chief faults, she felt, were the lack of creative and intellectual stimulation among teachers themselves; the tendency of union and management squabbles to interfere with the job of teaching; and a regimentation that leads to lack of individually tailored instruction.

Dana's solution was creative. Today she privately tutors learning disabled children. She has escaped the system which frustrated her but retained the part of the job she loved—working one-to-one with kids.

Dr. Baker suggests that persons who think they suffer from burn-out should analyze just what is bugging them, try to decide if their goals are being met, and admit it if they aren't. She suggests resorting to a therapist or career counsellor if talking with the boss and other less dramatic solutions don't suffice.

Other approaches both Baker and Montgomery suggest for burn-out victims are: developing formal or informal support groups with coworkers; perhaps switching to a different employer instead of a different career; keeping in good physical shape through exercise; and finding challenge in interests and hobbies outside of work.

Changing Jobs without Changing Employers

Mid-life career changes are becoming more common among employees and acceptable to employers. Changing technology has made many jobs obsolete and forced people to seek new careers. Recognizing this trend, a number of large corporations have developed job change programs as part of their personnel services functions, helping employees who want to change occupations, yet stay with the same employer. This benefits business because it cuts down on the cost of recruiting new employees.

At an Oregon manufacturer of electronic tools, informal opportunities for career counselling and mobility within the company have existed for many years. But since 1976, there has been a more formal program with human resources representatives who act as counsellors and referral agents for employees who wish to change jobs but remain at the company, according to an expert who has examined the program.

Employees who become dissatisfied with their jobs are encouraged to discuss their problems with their managers, take advantage of education and training programs, and, if necessary, use the services of career counsellors and/or human relations representatives to help them plan and prepare for their career change.

Analysis suggests that employees who use these resources most successfully are usually capable workers with adaptable personalities, who would be successful wherever they went to work.

How do managers react to employees who say they're not happy with their current job? Supportive, is the general rule, because managements recognize these people as the ones they don't want to lose. People who make job changes continue to learn on the job, tend not to become defensive or narrow-minded, and, generally, contribute creative ideas and solutions.

At a Connecticut insurance company there is a formal development appraisal process for employees who are in college graduate-level positions. There is a less formal process for clerical employees.

The worker who is bored with the job can go to a manager and say, "I like working for you, but . . ."; this leads to locating a new opportunity within the company. Career counselling is available from the personnel staff, and a tuition refund program can be used to prepare employees for lateral as well as upward moves.

The company also offers a continuing education program for clerical employees to help upgrade basic skills, as well as academic testing and career counselling to help formulate career plans. These plans may involve enrollment in such classes as English, English as a second language, mathematics, and typing.

Several companies have special programs for groups of employees with special needs, such as women, to help overcome traditional blocks to advancement. An Oregon company's Upward Mobility program is aimed at women and minorities, and there are also lunch-time career discussions for women and minority group members.

Why would a person want to change jobs but keep the same employer? Sometimes geography is a factor—the person may already work for the community's major employer. Or he or she may wish the convenience of keeping the same car pool arrangement or meeting friends for lunch each day. People who plan ahead to retirement may wish to remain in the same pension program; others may think that the stress that can accompany a job change will be lessened by keeping the same employer.

What if you work for a company that is large enough to offer other job opportunities but has no formal system for career changes?

One way is to use lunch hours and early or late hours to visit other parts of the company and meet people. Find out what they do and how they like it.

There are other ways to get to know people and the company: If something must be delivered to another department, volunteer; eat in the company cafeteria, even if the food is not your favorite; attend the company picnic and other group functions; and consider the company bowling or softball team if these are activities you enjoy.

Once you've found a department in the company that interests you, let your contacts know your interest in working with them. Find out what special training you need to do the job you'd like. If you decide to take classes to prepare yourself, don't be shy about reporting your progress.

And while promotions are always nice, don't be afraid of lateral moves, instead. Experts say these can be as rewarding as upward moves, and can give your career a new and exciting direction.

What You Do on Monday if You're Fired on Friday

It's five o'clock Friday afternoon and you have no plans for the weekend, nor for Monday morning either. You've been terminated, eliminated, fired. You have no job. If you're like most people, you'll be totally unprepared to cope with the change when Monday rolls around. Losing a job, especially when it's unexpected, is a major emotional shock.

Besides panic about where the next paycheck is coming from and the dangling feeling of being suddenly disconnected, you may inwardly sense some relief that your on-the-job problems have been solved, along with the numbness that follows shock, which makes it difficult for you to think or act on your own behalf.

Such "post-termination shock" can last for a week or a month, unless you prepare yourself in advance to deal with the effects and the problems of being suddenly unemployed. And today, this can happen to any of us for a variety of reasons: the effects of recession, loss of a company's market to overseas competitors, mergers, new technologies; the list is a long one. In general, being fired doesn't mean you've been a failure, just a victim.

What can you do *now* to prepare yourself for being jobless? First, read the warning signals at work. If the number of interesting new assignments suddenly dries up, if your boss is increasingly critical of your work, or people avoid meeting your eyes in the hall, this means trouble. If you're demoted, denied a promotion, or no longer invited to staff meetings, it's time to start making plans. And don't dismiss rumors. They are sometimes based on fact.

When the inevitable happens, you should keep in mind three points:

1. Find out why you're being let go.
2. Find out what rights and benefits you have.
3. Push for the best severance you can get.

Careful negotiating can affect your way of life for months to come, so don't walk out the door without attempting to arrange for: continuation of health or life insurance; taking severance pay over a period of a month or so, as if it were paychecks; good recommendations; and, if you've been laid off, the written promise that you'll be considered for the next jobs which will open up in your area. If you're a manager, you might ask for office space and outplacement assistance. But negotiate immediately; before the exit interview ends and you're on the outside.

Job termination is a subject governed by law. American common law used to regard employees as expendable commodities to be hired and fired at will. But, partially because of the increasing militancy of the work force, that viewpoint is changing. Fewer and fewer employees—from janitors to professors to managers over forty—are willing to "go quietly" if they consider themselves fired without fair cause. And courts are backing them up. In addition, there is the growing concept that job equity isn't something that a company can deprive you of lightly.

Yet, even if your present job seems secure, you should make a "doomsday" strategy plan now. It may one day save you from becoming a helpless victim adrift on the unemployment sea.

Start building a survival fund. You have to be able to make ends meet while you're looking for a job. It takes time to make contacts, wait for answers to ads and letters, set up interviews, and wait for decisions. In these days of inflation, most of us live from paycheck to paycheck, and it's hard to put anything away for that rainy day. But do it! Unemployment compensation is small and severance pay (if you get it) melts away faster than you can imagine.

Make a list of sources for temporary income. Doing some freelance work in your field or taking a part-time or temporary job may help tide you over financially until you get relocated. In the present economy, it may take months to find a new job in your field, especially if you work in seasonal or high-risk areas or if your job is subject to fluctuations in the economy.

Make contacts. There are people in your company, in your field, and in the service industries you work with, who may be able to help you if you're ever out of work. Cultivate them for future referrals and even job openings.

Prepare for a possible career change. Being terminated may be the best time for you to update your job prospects or to switch careers altogether. So look ahead. Take courses to increase your competence or expertise in your present job or start to work toward a major career change while you're still employed.

No one likes to think about getting fired. But avoiding the subject only makes matters worse when it happens, especially in the current economy. A little forethought now may save you a lot of anxiety later and will help you build a solid base of operations from which to look for your next job. For your own sake, start right now to develop a game plan for dealing with dismissal.

Six Tips on Starting Your New Job

You're due to report for your first day on the new job. So, naturally enough, you're feeling nervous. Maybe you're straight out of school, and this is your first "real world" job. Perhaps you've relocated and are trying to learn about a new city, a new boss, and new colleagues, all at once. You might have switched careers, in which case you're wondering what this new future holds. Maybe you've had to spend several months out of work, and you've begun to wonder if you can hold down any job at all.

Your nervousness is natural, but don't let it get out of hand. After all, you were nervous before your interview, too, but you did convince the company to hire you. If they hadn't thought you were qualified, you'd still be job-hunting. So you know that on paper, at least, you've got the credentials your employer is looking for. And your manner and dress must have impressed the interviewer too.

So, tip number one for your first day of work is: Dress for success again. Until you have figured out what your new company's "style" is, better leave your favorite, most individualistic outfit in the closet. Though you've been hired for your competence, you will also be expected to fit in.

At the beginning you're going to have to operate in a blur of new faces, new names, and new procedures; and you're going to make mistakes. Tip two: Your coworkers and supervisors know this; and they're going to help you acclimate yourself. After all, easing your uncertainties, creating a favorable attitude toward the company, avoiding factors that might cause future misunderstandings, and communicating a company's goal to its new employees is what orientation is all about— or what it should be, if companies want to reduce costly employee turnover and hang onto good employees (like you) during the first few critical weeks.

Consider the following examples. After being wined and dined and told that the company really prized its new graduates, Lisa S. was thrown into her first project without much briefing and with little help from coworkers. Her boss, the one person who might have been able to help her adapt, was too busy to take the time; no one else seemed to care. So, after a couple of months, Lisa moved to another firm. The company lost a potentially valuable employee *and* the money it had spent to recruit her. What's more, it had to begin the slow, expensive recruitment process all over again.

On the other hand, George B. signed on with an industrial firm right after he graduated from a technical institute. He was immediately taken in charge by his supervisor, given a tour of the plant, and introduced around. Personnel showed him a filmstrip designed to ease his transition into the company work force and even assigned him a "buddy" who could answer questions about pay, sick leave, and insurance and share the lunch hour with him. From time to time, the personnel office called him to check on his progress. Meanwhile, his boss worked closely with him, gradually assigning him more and more responsibility. George couldn't be happier in his job. And, thanks to advice he got from his "buddy," he is planning to take a company-subsidized night course in computer programming.

In order to help new employees succeed on the job, forward-thinking organizations are supplementing their "welcome to" booklets with a variety of information, including maps, multimedia presentations, and informal meetings with company people. One major telecommunications company, for example, starts off by briefing new male craftworkers that the company will not tolerate harassment of women coworkers. According to one personnel officer there, "If you get people started with the idea that the company isn't going to tolerate specific kinds of behavior, it saves a lot of grief later."

Unlike Lisa S.'s former employer, smart companies use orientation as a time to provide extensive background information to their workers, give preliminary on-the-job training, anticipate and eliminate problems before they start, and generally make new workers feel enthusiastic about their jobs, reduce turnover, and promote good attitudes in their employees.

When you report for work, what can you do to make the most of whatever orientation is provided? Tip three: Observe the company's working style—how things are done—and try to fit in from the start. Some places operate very formally, for example, and "by the book." Others are conspicuously informal, friendly, and "laid back." Since people know that you've got a whole set of procedures to learn, take advantage of their willingness to help out by asking for advice and feedback.

Tip four: Develop relationships carefully. You're going to run into office politics sooner or later, for example, but be sure to put off taking sides until you know the whole picture. Try to develop friendly relationships with all your coworkers, not just the ones you think may be useful. And while you can't ask, "Will you be my mentor?" in so many words, start right away to find supervisors or coworkers who can take you under their wings, if no "buddy system" or other way is available.

Tip five: Keep a log of projects assigned to you and the dates on which you completed them, or other ongoing evidence of your performance. You'll both encourage yourself and provide your superiors with useful information for evaluation and salary reviews.

One last tip to remember before you start work: Orienting yourself to a new job is just like finding one. If you want to succeed, you have to go all out.

PRACTICAL ASPECTS OF WORKING

Even if you've worked for years, chances are that you aren't really familiar with many of the practical aspects of being an employee. Sure, you've read the memos Personnel sends around. And you're glad of the new dental plan. Maybe you're considering the company's offer to send you through Smokenders. But as a smart employee you should investigate all your benefits and rights instead of lumping them all together and assuming that you'll deal with problems as they come up . . . and hope that they don't.

Employees who examine their benefits may be in for a surprise. For one thing, benefit patterns are changing. At some companies, it's now possible to choose what benefits you want from a sort of "benefit cafeteria." Some of the choices: extra time off, "wellness" medical plans, added insurance.

With two-career families on the increase, many companies are taking a hard look at another benefit: child care. In some cases, they're extending parental leaves or even providing day-care centers.

And then there's the question of productivity. Would rewards make you try even harder? Some companies are instituting that. On the other end of the scale, look at discrimination. What if you suddenly discover that the man (or woman) in the next office is making more than you for the same kind of work? And do you know what to do if you and a forklift collide, or if you slip on ice near the loading docks?

Don't worry that you're being greedy. After all, you work in a business. As an employee, your business isn't just to do the job for which you were hired, but also to put your own, personal business of being Company X's employee on a firm, informed footing.

10
Getting What You've Earned

New Fringe Benefits for New Mothers . . . and Fathers

Many companies and unions are now establishing policies that recognize the desire of women to return to work shortly after giving birth. There is also a growing trend toward recognizing the right of workers to take a leave of absence to care for a newborn child and this is being made available to men as well as women.

Why would a man take time off from work to care for an infant? In some cases he'd like some time away from work while the wife may be in the midst of a developing career. Other times his employer may be more generous than hers in arranging a leave for this purpose. And for some couples it is the husband who wants to stay home with the young child and the wife who prefers to return to work. Some women have higher paying jobs than their husbands, and this makes the wife's return to work more practical, even if her husband has to take an unpaid leave of absence.

Mutual of New York offers all employees a six-month leave without pay if they wish to stay at home with a newborn child, says Jean Doyle of that insurance company's personnel benefits department. To avoid discrimination, the benefit is offered to both men and women.

At a midwestern manufacturing company, the reasoning for "parental" leave policy is somewhat different. A survey, according to one spokesperson, showed that good day-care facilities were available for youngsters from six months up. So it offers six-month leaves of absence (without pay) to either parent who wishes to stay home to care for a child during this period.

The American Federation of Teachers (AFT) has a national policy of encouraging its over 2,000 local unions to include parental leave as a benefit in its labor contracts. Many locals are including this clause in their contracts. AFT's employees may take five days paid parental leave when the child is born and up to a year's unpaid leave without losing benefits, seniority, or their job. Members of the New Orleans Federation of Teachers, an AFT bargaining unit, may take a year's maternity or paternity leave for birth or adoption of a baby. For the first eighty-nine days of the leave the parent is paid the difference between his or her salary and that paid to a substitute; then, extended maternity leave without pay may be taken until the end of one year. This is considered part of the union's "personal or medical necessity" leave clause.

In Chicago, AFT Local #1 members may take ten days paid leave for the birth of a baby or adoption of a child under five years old. After this paid time, both men and women are entitled to five months of unpaid leave.

AFT's leadership in this area is attributable to two factors: Because there are so many women in the teaching profession, the members are sympathetic to the need for men to take an increased role in child-rearing responsibility; on the other hand, as more men become teachers, there is a need to make the child-care benefit apply to them.

There is a need to distinguish between the physical recovery of the new mother and time for caring for an infant in determining the relevance of the Civil Rights Act to what has been traditionally called maternity leave. Once a woman has physically recovered from pregnancy and giving birth, under the law she is considered to be on child-rearing leave, rather than disability.

It is at this point that a father's entitlement to equal benefits comes into effect. If a mother is allowed the option of taking, say, six months to stay home with her child after her physician says she is physically able to work and if her company has a specific policy about paid or unpaid leave during this time, about holding a job open for her and/or continuing fringe benefits and seniority rights, a man is entitled to the same treatment.

Equal treatment, rather than special treatment, applies to a new parent's request for child-rearing leave. If a company grants leave for an employee to return to school or to leave temporarily to care for a terminally ill parent in a distant city, it should also have to consider child rearing a legitimate personal leave. A company without a history of such a policy would probably not be held responsible for granting such a leave.

How many fathers are taking "child care" leave? Will corporate compliance with the Civil Rights Act in offering both men and women the option of time off for early parenting encourage a new trend? Little solid information has been gathered to date. If there is a trend, it is just beginning, and the large number of women who return to work shortly after childbirth, plus the increasing interest shown by men in caring for children (including joint and paternal custody of children and single parent adoptions) will probably encourage this trend.

For information on your company's policies regarding parental leave, contact your personnel or union office.

What's New in Day Care?

Mothers with children under the age of three are joining the employment ranks faster than any other group, according to the Women's Bureau of the U.S. Department of Labor. Whether the reason these women join the labor force is economic survival or personal preference, they all face the same problem: Who's going to take care of the children?

For some women, a nearby relative, such as a retired grandparent, is the answer. For others, staggered work hours so that one parent works a different shift from the other keeps the responsibility for child care within the family. But the vast majority of women who work (and fathers who are bringing up their children) must make other arrangements for child care.

The range of possibilities is wide—a hired babysitter who comes to the home; a babysitter to whose home the child is brought; a "day-care mother," who cares for several children in her home either with a license from the state or on a more informal basis; or a day-care center.

When one New York organization advertises for employees, it notes that one of the benefits it offers is child-care referrals. It provides to new hirees a booklet of babysitters in the area, compiled from suggestions made by employees. People interested in such services can check their references, discuss fees and other arrangements. Prospective employees are advised to investigate child-care possibilities before they start work.

The Department of Labor in Washington, D.C., began its own day-care center for young children of employees in 1968 as a demonstration project. Today the center continues as an incorporated non-profit parent cooperative, with the owner/users forming the governing board, hiring the staff, and setting policy. The government, as the employer, provides the space.

Like any other employer, the Department of Labor wishes to raise morale and reduce turnover, so it started a child-care center in the way many companies have done. The Labor Department had the added interest of showing other employers that child care on the job can work.

Perhaps the most ambitious effort in company day care is in Texas, where a manufacturer of medical apparatus recently dedicated a 260-child day-care center at its 1000-employee plant.

The center's director, who supervises a staff of forty child-care employees (including substitutes), says it charges a nominal fee. The center accepts children from six weeks to five years old and includes a kindergarten. Parents of older children are on their own for after-school care arrangements; there would be too many children to set up a program for them. This benefit helps attract potential employees, according to the personnel director.

Parents who use the center come from all areas of the company—housekeeping staff, manufacturing, and executives. Some employees, who could afford private child care, choose instead to use the company program, where the emphasis is on quality education, staffing at a higher level than required by law, nourishing snacks and lunches, and the convenience of having child care at the place of work.

Most single parents or two-career couples who must find care for children are more likely to find group or individual care in the community than care supplied by their employer. A growing number of nursery schools offer extended day programs for working parents, and there are many private day care centers—some of them operating as commercial chains or franchises—in addition to the non-profit centers that have been formed in some communities.

Many women who are primarily homemakers care for the children of working mothers; often they are found by word of mouth. "I mentioned to the Avon lady that I need a full-time sitter because I was returning to work," said a school psychologist. "She introduced me to her mother, who took the job."

Other resources for locating individuals or group child-care facilities include the secretary of the elementary school in your area, nursery schools, YWCAs, women's groups, and college placement offices.

Finding good child care can be a lot like finding a good job. It takes a lot of imagination, investigation, and careful thought. But millions of working parents are finding it can be done and are meeting the needs of both children and parents.

Taking Time for a Vacation

Why are vacations important to you?

Do you feel it's necessary to get away from your working environment, or are you a workaholic who hates leaving the office . . . even for a brief rest? Are you nervous and restless during a vacation, counting the hours until you can get back to work, or do you, instead, count the days until that vacation begins?

Ten thousand readers of *Psychology Today* responded to a survey about why they take vacations. Managers, administrators, and other business persons constitute twenty-one percent of the sample. They are followed by a group of teachers, counsellors, social workers, and nurses, twenty percent; professionals who hold advanced degrees, eleven percent; white collar workers, eleven percent; students, ten percent; technicians and other skilled workers, six percent; semiskilled workers, three percent; with the rest including artists, writers, craftsmen, housewives, and others.

While forty percent are married, forty-six percent are single or divorced. Men comprise forty percent and women sixty percent of the sample. Incomes under $15,000 are reported by twenty-four percent, while another twenty-nine percent earn between $15,000 and $24,999. Almost half are under age thirty.

The most frequently cited reason for taking a vacation is the need to relax. The majority of those who give this reason are in their thirties and have responsible and stressful jobs.

The second most mentioned reason for vacationing is for enriching one's life via learning or spiritual enhancement, investigating places they have never seen. Many of the respondents who cite this reason are between thirty and forty-nine years old and are the group least likely to be bored at home, according to data. Not only is work important to this group, but also it's something which they enjoy very much, according to the *Psychology Today* survey.

The opportunity to spend time with one's family, "to get to know children better, and to visit friends or relatives," is another major response. With work only moderately important to those who list this reason, seventy-six percent of them describe themselves as very or moderately happy at home. They are also found to be among those who look forward the most to returning home after a vacation.

Those who report enjoying their vacations the most look for excitement, exotic adventure, danger, new friends, and sexual escapades, according to the magazine. Most of these respondents are single and young. The data show that while males are in the majority, they are only slightly more likely than women to want such thrills.

If your motivation for vacationing is the desire to "find" yourself, to work out personal problems, or to be alone to relax, then you are like the "self-discovery" respondents of this sampling. This group reports enjoying work the least and describes it as "relatively unimportant." Usually among the youngest respondents, they are more frequently employed in low-level jobs and bored with their work.

The last major reason for vacationing is the need to escape one's routine. Women fall into this category in significantly greater numbers, as do persons under twenty-five years of age. Highly ambivalent about work and leisure, the people in this group want the best of both worlds with the least amount of effort, the article notes.

A significant finding of the survey is that few of us really change while on vacation. Thus, if you're a workaholic you only transfer your compulsion to a new locale.

Which sex enjoys vacationing the most? Women derive more enjoyment from their vacations, as well as in spending money while taking time off from work. But women also place greater importance on work. While men are more eager to return to work, they have a stronger belief about their entitlement to vacations.

Regarding the amount of vacation time, nearly half of the group believe they get as much time as they deserve. Length of vacation time by respondents ranged as follows: six percent had no time off; fourteen percent reported one week; twenty-five percent had two weeks; twenty percent took vacation time of three weeks; sixteen percent took four to five-week vacations; while another sixteen percent said six or more weeks. These figures were compared to the national percentages from the *Travel Market Yearbook, 1980*. That year twenty-eight percent of the nation took no vacation; seventeen percent had a week off; twenty-four percent reported two weeks of vacation time; ten percent had three-week vacations; twelve percent, between four and five weeks; and nine percent of the nation had vacations lasting six weeks or more.

Whether you spend your vacation sailing the seas or repainting your living room, consider how a change of pace from your regular routine can bring new vitality to the job.

Employee's Rights—a Growing Concern

In 1976, a supervisor for a major telecommunications company was fired two weeks after participating in a May Day rally. He brought the company to court on the grounds that he was wrongfully and unconstitutionally let go for his political beliefs.

The company initially argued that he was dismissed for criminal misconduct since he had been arrested for attacking police at the demonstration. It later maintained that a private employer is not required to employ persons who advocate a position contrary to the best interests of the employer. The supervisor lost the case on the basis of the common law in New York and in most other states, which stipulates that an employee can be dismissed "for good cause, for no cause, or even for cause morally wrong."

In his appeal, his lawyer argued that an employee's right to free speech is threatened if he can be fired for exercising that right. He lost the appeal. However, his case and others that have arisen under "employee rights" reflect a growing concern about protecting the jobs of the three-quarters of the nation's non-union private work force. Employees today are bringing lawsuits against employers with such diverse charges as invasion of privacy, unlawful discrimination, and breaking implicit contracts.

The Connecticut Supreme Court, for example, ruled in favor of a frozen-food plant employee who was fired simply for protesting to his superiors that less meat was being put in entrees than the labels indicated. In California, an employee who was discharged for refusing to commit perjury, won the case against his employer. A woman who claimed she was dismissed from her clerical job for a city housing commission because she is white was recently awarded $750,000 by a jury in the second trial of her case. And, an employee who developed the basic concept for a product widely sold by his company took it to court and won the right to receive profits from such sales.

While there are no figures indicating how many lawsuits are being brought against employers to uphold the rights of workers, companies are being forced to respond to the issues if for no other reason than to avoid the expense involved in litigation and to help prevent union activity. Programs to train managers how to better deal with employees, seminars on employees' rights, the establishment of personnel programs, and affirmative action manuals which outline company policy, are some examples of what companies are doing to keep employees satisfied and ward off legal hassles.

Wells Fargo & Co., San Francisco, has set up a training program aimed at helping supervisors learn how to deal with race and sex bias, what to do about employees who are not performing well, and how to build employee self-esteem.

Another company, Southern Bancorporation of Alabama, now has a policy under which no one may be fired on the spot, so that there is time for investigating an employee problem and giving it the careful consideration it deserves.

Citibank in New York goes a step further in allowing due process for any employee with a gripe. The bank has set up a hearing procedure for workers who want to issue a complaint about a written reprimand or firing. They can appeal to a "problem review board," which consists of three employees, a personnel executive, and a bank vice-president. The panel hears the case, then makes a recommendation to a senior bank executive who makes the final determination.

Despite efforts by companies to improve employer-employee relations, there is resistance to the notion that an employee, disgruntled with the way he or she is being treated, can call upon the law for help in what many employers see as their private domain. A management consultant on employee rights estimates that only a few hundred of the 20,000 companies in the U.S. with 500 or more employees are acting to improve relations. Part of the problem is that while judges are willing to hear cases, the law which gives employers the option to fire someone is still on the books. In addition, if the law were changed, there is concern that courts would be overburdened with cases difficult to prove.

Regardless of potential pitfalls, more and more companies are responding to complaints of employees in order to keep their "open doors" from turning into revolving doors.

An authority on the subject suggests there are three basic ways employees can go about issuing a grievance: (1) if you're a union member, your specific grievance may be addressed within a collective bargaining agreement; (2) regulatory statutes that fall within the jurisdiction of EEO, OSHA, ERISA, or some other government agency may cover your particular grievance; if so, the complaint should be brought to the attention of the appropriate agency; (3) private litigation is another means to protect civil or contractual rights as an employee.

As more and more employees bring their grievances to light, signs appear hopeful for a working environment which is more considerate of worker's rights.

Benefiting from the Fringes

Perhaps your salary hasn't increased as much as the cost of living in the past few years. But what about your fringe benefits? For many American workers, the value of fringe benefits has improved at a faster pace than the size of their actual paycheck. Even if you're not receiving any new benefits, your employer is probably spending more to continue your old ones.

The cost of benefits has been growing almost twice as fast as wages. Part of this increase may be explained by the increase in the cost of medical care and consequently of health insurance, a benefit frequently provided by employers. Pension costs continue to grow, too, because a pension is usually based on an employee's last few years' salary, which is generally higher than his or her earlier work years.

The cost to employers of time not worked but paid for—coffee breaks, lunch hours, and paid holidays and vacations—is also greater as wages increase. This is also true of the Social Security tax, which is based on a percentage of a person's salary.

Employers are not adding as many new benefits as they were a few years ago when the economy was better; but where new benefits are being added, the most growth is in insurance benefits, according to one expert. Dental insurance is probably increasing the most rapidly. Other observers have noted an increase in legal insurance (prepaid legal plans, entitling the person to a certain amount of services by a lawyer during each year). Eye-care benefits are also becoming more popular.

The most lavish fringes have been found in the petroleum industry, followed by public utilities and the chemical industry. The lowest cost-fringe packages were offered by hospitals, department stores, and textile products and apparel manufacturers.

Among the factors influencing the cost of the fringe package is the average length of vacation. For the petroleum industry this was sixteen days per year, and for the textile products and apparel industry it was eight days.

Many employers cite union pressure as a reason for expanding benefit programs; other businesses become more generous in an effort to attract or retain employees. The Electronics Association of California, for example, found that many of the state's small electronics firms had been increasing their benefits because of a labor shortage.

Some companies offer fringe benefits that reflect the employer's line of business, such as free air travel for airline employees or discounts on purchases for department store workers. Others reflect special concerns of management. Hallmark Cards, Pitney Bowes, IBM Corp., and Foote, Cone & Belding (an advertising agency) offer their employees adoption benefits to help employees with this often costly process.

While many fringe benefits are aimed at helping employees to live better, two unions have negotiated the right to special care should they develop a terminal illness. Payment for hospice care (a facility that specializes in the care of terminally ill patients) is guaranteed as part of their union contract.

If you are thinking of changing jobs, don't forget to consider fringe benefits and what they mean to you and your family. A dental plan that includes orthodontic coverage means a lot to a family with several pre-teen-age children. Long vacations are valuable if you can afford to travel. And a subsidized cafeteria is of no value if you prefer to bring your own lunch.

Whether you are a new employee or a long-time job holder, be sure you understand what benefits are offered by your employer. Find out who is in charge of administering the benefit plan, and don't be afraid to ask questions. Fringes are really an important part of your paycheck, so be sure you take advantage of all benefits for which you qualify.

New Law Attracts Interest in Flexible Benefits Programs

A few years from now, when perhaps you'll change jobs, you may be in for a surprise when your new employer discusses the company's benefits package. Instead of telling you what benefits are offered, you may be asked which benefits you would find most suitable to your needs. You may have a choice, for example, of choosing between a few extra days' vacation, a matching savings plan, or increased medical benefits.

A federal law now makes it easier for companies to offer employees a choice of benefits which best suit their needs. Companies can now offer you a three-way trade-off between cash, benefits, and deferred compensation, such as pension plans. Only a handful of firms and the state of Alaska now offer these plans, but many others intend to start flexible benefit plans soon. Flexible benefits will offer you a broad range of choices; and if you work for a company that offers such a program, you will be required to do some extra work to decide on the best plan for you.

Many compensation experts believe that flexible compensation plans, also known as "cafeteria-style" benefits programs because they allow you to "do it your way," will become a widespread trend in the future. Here is some information that will help you if you work for a company which has such a program.

What is Flexible Compensation?   One definition: It is a system under which each individual has some choice of the different types of total compensation allowed him or her. The concept is not new. Many employers now provide optional coverages at an extra cost, such as life insurance or long-term disability, in addition to their basic benefit program. But new tax laws make it possible for you to opt for a larger amount of life insurance and extensive medical coverage over profit sharing or extra vacation if you have a large family. Or if your spouse works at another company where extensive employee benefits are provided, you may feel little need for medical and death benefit protection but have a great interest in savings and extra vacation. If you are close to retirement, you may value pension benefits more highly than other coverages.

How Does the Program Work?   Under most flexible plans, your employer will establish a core benefit program which is applied uniformly to all employees. For example, your company may offer the minimum level of coverage on group life insurance, pension benefits, medical insurance, disability benefits, and vacation time. You are then given a certain number of credits based on your age, length of service, and salary level and can choose benefits which meet your specific needs or preferences.

Employees who work at companies with these programs are more satisfied with them than with traditional compensation plans, according to some experts. Employees have reported they are pleased to know exactly how much money the company is spending for them in benefits and that they can exercise some choice in how it is spent.

Your company will benefit from the program for several reasons. Many employees choose to work for a company because of the benefits program it offers. Companies have found "flex plans" help attract employees. Benefit costs can be controlled because benefits only go to those employees who want them. And, perhaps most importantly, employees who are more satisfied with their company are more productive. So, advocates of the program say, companies get more for their money.

If you work for a company which has a flex program, you probably will be required to study carefully the different benefits offered to determine the best package for you. But your company should provide a lot of help. Some of the methods companies have used to inform employees about their flex programs are: internal memos, a bimonthly newsletter, a direct mail campaign, a brochure and looseleaf handbook, administrative training sessions, one-on-one counselling opportunities, videotape programs, and more.

When American Can Co., based in Greenwich, CT, initiated its program in 1978, it found that employees were quite willing to spend time on making their benefits decisions: Each employee spent an average of eight hours on the task. One employee, commenting on the information program, said, "What it really did was to educate me. In most companies they don't have choices. They just hum right through the benefits program when you join and that's it."

Some have expressed doubt if employees have the necessary judgment to make sound choices if offered a flexible benefits program. But a spokesman from American Can, obviously a proponent of the program, says: "Companies trust their employees to spend their salaries, don't they? What is so different about trusting them with their benefits?"

And, a number of compensation experts are convinced that flexible compensation is the trend of the future. Says one: "It is not a question of *whether* it will come, but *when*."

If you are interested in a flexible benefits program, you should check with your company personnel department to see if it is considering implementing one. Such programs require a great deal of effort on the part of the company and employee alike to implement. Your role in the program's implementation will be to educate yourself as much as possible on the pros and cons of each benefit to determine the most beneficial package for you.

Incentive Awards Add Income

A bookkeeper in a specialty shop, Marge is flaunting a crisp new $100 bill, her incentive bonus for a recent cost-cutting suggestion. Her idea—if the shop discontinued its long-time practice of billing customers even when no balance is due on their accounts, the savings would be significant—made her the first winner in the shop's new incentive plan.

Hal's a winner, too. He quit smoking and got a bonus for doing it. His health-conscious employer also provides nutritious free lunches for employees and a gym for them and their families, all because he's convinced that healthy workers produce more and have lower absentee rates.

Lee got a fat check for increasing personal productivity. Her job in an electronic assembly shop kept Lee on her feet all day. Fatigue was slowing her down. She began using a high stool which allowed her to sit for about twenty minutes of every hour. Standing on a carpet sample with padding underneath further reduced fatigue. With the worst behind her, Lee was able to pace herself and increase her average production thirteen percent. Seeing her bonus check made her coworkers try harder, too.

Using financial incentives to increase motivation is nothing new. Industry has always used formal incentives (money, bonuses, promotion, and special privileges) and informal ones (praise, encouragement, minimum supervision). Negative incentives (reprimands, disciplinary action, and layoffs, for example) aren't unusual either.

Until recently, salary increases and attractive benefit packages were expected to keep workers' motivation and production high. With workers' attitudes changing, traditional incentives tend to be taken for granted. That fact, as well as drops in productivity, forced management to rethink incentives.

Taking a closer look at Marge, Hal, and Lee shows how different incentive plans can be. Some reward cost cutting; some focus on increased productivity; others reward workers' health consciousness.

The plan of one Illinois company rewards *anything* that helps improve company profits including:

- increases in productivity
- savings in material and supplies
- better use of plant and equipment
- increases in sales.

This plan also penalizes slippages in productivity, waste, lost time, and customer rejects. It works this way: For every dollar of net sales, sixty-five cents is allowed for *all* manufacturing costs—materials, supplies, labor, fringe benefits, machine rent or depreciation, maintenance, utilities, etc. When costs drop, savings are split 50–50 with employees. Bonuses are based on employees' base earnings and are paid monthly. Regular statements show net billings and manufacturing costs for the past four months; the plant superintendent explains why some figures have changed. The plan is successful, in part, because it keeps employees informed about what's going on.

At a lumber company in Minneapolis, the "Well Plan" rewards employees with free fruit for snacks and nutritious lunches. Since employees started receiving two hours' extra pay each month for not being absent or late, absenteeism has dropped to three percent (compared to an average of four percent for their industry). Cigarette machines were removed and coffee machines dispense only decaf, but nothing is forced on workers. The policy is to present healthier alternatives.

These programs reward employees on a regular basis, but not all work that way. A one-shot award of $500 to $2,000 for a well-done project or activity can be a very effective motivator, say psychologists, provided the reward is delivered promptly.

If your company has no incentive plan, why not work through your employee organization, supervisor, or union rep to get a plan started? Though some companies are traditionally slow to adopt new programs, management might be willing to give the idea a three-month trial. As productivity soars, so do the chances for implementing incentives on a long-term basis. That could put more money in your pocket soon.

Workers' Compensation
—When You Get Hurt on the Job

If you slam your fingers in the file cabinet, sprain your ankle at a construction site, or break your arm tripping in the typing pool, there's a good chance you won't have to suffer financial worry along with your pain.

Because, if you work in an office, factory, project, or store, you're probably covered by Workers' Compensation, a state-run insurance plan that entitles you to medical and income benefits if you're hurt on the job or incur an industrial disease.

If you've been fortunate, you may never have heard of Workers' Compensation. Only when people have an accident do they find out about this no-fault plan that compensates them when they suffer on-the-job injuries. Then Workers' Compensation can pay your doctor and hospital bills, give you up to $426 a week in tax-free disability income while you convalesce and pay partial disability even when you return to work. It will also pay to train you for a new job if your injuries prevent you from handling the old one.

John McH., for example, was a foreman in a carpet warehouse and happened to be standing in the way when a storage rack collapsed sending huge rolls of heavy carpets cascading to the floor. One of the rolls struck John and pinned him to the floor.

It was a bad accident that well might have killed him, but he survived. As it was, he was laid up with multiple fractures for six months and was unable to go back to his regular work in the warehouse when he recovered. Luckily, Workers' Compensation helped John and his family weather the financial storm by paying his hospital and medical bills. During the months without work it also paid him about two-thirds of his regular salary and when he was up and around again, paid the bill to retrain him for work in the office in a less physically demanding job.

Workers' Compensation is not just for the victims of severe accidents, however. Alison S. sprained her back lifting heavy book boxes in her sixth-grade classroom. Workers' Compensation paid her doctor's bill and the weekly therapy she needed until she was well. Then there was Janet K. She cut her arm on a jagged piece of broken packing crate in the stockroom of the factory where she worked. Workers' Compensation paid for the hospital emergency room and an allowance for the few days she had to stay home.

In addition to medical and salary compensation, many Workers' Compensation plans provide for other benefits, too, such as travel expenses for medical treatment; injury, death, and pension benefits for dependents; and, as in the case of John McH., the cost of vocational rehabilitation.

Though it may be new to many people, Workers' Compensation has been around since the turn of the century. (It used to be called *Workmen's* Compensation until the women's movement reminded the government that they get hurt on the job, too.) In those early days, a man injured at work had to rely on the generosity of the boss or sue him for negligence and, failing that, fall back on charity to support his family.

Slowly, state by state, government stepped in with assistance. Now all fifty states have Workers' Compensation plans. They differ slightly from one another in administration and benefits. Some are secured by state insurance funds, others by private insurance companies; but all plans must meet federal Labor Department standards. In most states, the employee pays nothing for his benefits; the employer bears the whole cost. Other states require a small employee contribution. Changes in the plans are continuous. In one recent year, nearly 200 new laws were passed relative to these programs. Today, sixty million workers are covered by Workers' Compensation benefits in the average week.

Though a boon to people who work, the system does have some drawbacks. It doesn't cover all workers. Benefits are not up to recommended minimums in some states. Until recently, victims of occupational disease have not been getting appropriate attention.

How to Qualify for Workers' Compensation When you are injured on the job, you should inquire immediately about your company's participation in Workers' Compensation and how you can qualify for benefits. Here are some steps you should follow to make sure you meet all benefit requirements and some places to go for more information.

- No matter how insignificant your injury may seem at the time, report it to your supervisor. This will help substantiate that the injury happened on the job . . . especially if you run into late-developing complications.

- Report your accident promptly. The sooner you let Workers' Compensation representatives know the problem, the easier and faster it will be to receive benefits.
- Ask for an accident report and fill it out at once.
- Make photocopies of all forms or statements you complete.
- Check to find out exactly what expenses are covered. Alison learned quite by chance that transportation costs to the therapist were eligible.
- Keep a log of all appointments, treatments, discussions, and other information pertinent to your injury.

Because Workers' Compensation benefits and rules vary from state to state, it is impossible to give more than superficial details in this article. To find out exactly what your state plan covers, and how to file for a claim when you do have an accident, you or a member of your family should contact one or more of the following sources for information: your union or other employee group; your employer's Workers' Compensation insurance company; the Workers' Compensation commission in your state.

A Careers Bibliography

It is said that one of the characteristics of this information age into which we are moving is that getting ahead will require continuing self-education. This is already true in terms of careers. Within recent years a whole new genre of career-oriented literature has been published, of which the book you're reading is one example.

The following pages list a number of other books that may be of value to you in holding the job you have, moving on or up to a better one, and understanding more about the employment world. Some are already classics in the field, others are recent publications; both are well worth looking into.

In addition, some organizations have been listed which can be sources for specific information that is not in book form, but may be available in pamphlets or similar literature.

There's a great deal here to help you expand your career horizons. Use it well.

General References for Fields, Careers, Training, etc.

Angel, J.L. *Directory of Foreign Firms Operating in the U.S.* New York: World Trade Academy Press, 1978.

Colgate, Craig, Jr., ed. *National Trade & Professional Associations of the United States and Canada and Labor Unions*. Columbia Books, Inc., annual publ.

Encyclopedia of Associations (3 vols.). Detroit: Gale Research Company Book Tower.

International Association of Counseling Services, Inc. *Directory of Counseling Services*. Washington, D.C.: annual publ.

Klein, Bernard, ed. *Guide to American Directories*. Coral Springs, Fla.: B. Klein Publications, 1978.

National Center for Public Service Internship Programs. *A Directory of Public Service Internship Opportunities for the Graduate, Post-Graduate, and Mid-Career Professional*. Washington, D.C.: 1976.

National Home Study Council; 1601 18 St., N.W., Washington, D.C.

Norback, Craig T. *The Careers Encyclopedia*. Homewood, IL: Dow Jones-Irwin, 1980.

Renryzky, A., ed. *Directory of Internships, Work Experience Programs and On-the-Job Training Opportunities*. Thousand Oaks, CA: Ready Reference Press, 1978.

Wasserman, Paul, ed. *Training and Development Organizations Directory*. Detroit: Gale Research Company Book Tower, 1978.

Books and Organizations to Help You Choose a Career

(Directed primarily to high school and college students and recent grads)

American Council of Education. *Quarterly Directory*. Washington, D.C.

Bachhuber, T.D., and Harwood, R.K. *Directions: A Guide to Career Planning*. Boston: Houghton Mifflin Co., 1978.

Bennet, R.L. *Careers through Cooperative Work Experience*. New York: John Wiley & Sons, 1977.

Council for Non-Collegiate Continuing Education, 6 N. Sixth St., Richmond, VA.

Erdlen, J.D., and Sweet, D. *Job Hunting for the College Graduate*. Washington, D.C.: Heath, 1979.

Hopke, W.E., ed. *The Encyclopedia of Careers and Vocational Guidance*. Chicago: J.G. Ferguson Publishing, 1978.

Lederer, Muriel. *The Guide to Career Education*. New York: Quadrangle, 1974.

Lobb, C. *Exploring Careers through Volunteerism*. New York: Richard Rosen Press, Inc., 1976.

Manpower Research Associates. *ARCO Handbook of Job and Career Opportunities*. New York: ARCO Publishing, 1978.

United States Department of Labor, Bureau of Labor Statistics. *Occupational Outlook Handbook*. Washington, D.C.: annual publ.

Books to Help You Find a Job

Biegeleisen, J.I. *Job Résumés—How to Write Them, How to Present Them, Preparing for Interviews*. New York: Grosset & Dunlap, 1976.

Bolles, R.N. *What Color is Your Parachute? A Practical Manual for Job Hunters and Career Changers*. Berkeley, CA: Ten Speed Press, 1979.

Corwen, L. *Your Résumé: Key to a Better Job*. New York: Arco Publishing, 1976.

Fox, M. *Put Your Degree to Work: A Career-Planning and Job-Hunting Guide for the New Professional*. New York: W.W. Norton, 1979.

Greco, B. *How to Get the Job That's Right for You*. Homewood, IL: Dow Jones–Irwin, 1975.

Irish, R.K. *Go Hire Yourself an Employer*. New York: Anchor Books, 1973.

Johansen, N. *Write Your Ticket to Success—A Do-It-Yourself Guide to Effective Résumé Writing and Job Hunting*. Annapolis, MD: Job Hunters Forum (GP Enterprises), 1976.

Lathrop, R. *Who's Hiring Who*. Berkeley, CA: Ten Speed Press, 1977.

Stanat, K. and Reardon, P. *Job Hunting Secrets and Tactics*. Chicago: Follett/Westwind, 1977.

Sweet, D. *The Job Hunter's Manual*. Reading, MA: Addison–Wesley, 1975

Thompson, M.R. *Why Should I Hire You? How to Get the Job You Really Want*. New York: Jove Publications, 1975.

Ulrich, Heinz and Connor, J. Robert. *The National Job Finding Guide*. Garden City, NY: Doubleday/Dolphin, 1981.

Yeomans, W.N. *Jobs '79—Where They Are, How to Get Them*. New York: Berkley Publishing, 1978.

Books to Help You Develop Your Career

Coulson, Robert. *The Termination Handbook*. New York: MacMillan, 1981.

Djeddah, E. *Moving Up—How to Get High-Salaried Jobs*. Berkeley, CA: Ten Speed Press, 1978.

DuBrin, Andre J. *Survival in the Office: How to Move Ahead or Hang On*. New York: Van Nostrand Reinhold, 1977.

Haldane, B. *Career Satisfaction and Success—A Guide to Job Freedom*. New York: AMACOM, 1974.

Howard, John; Cunningham, David; and Rechnitzer, Peter. *Rusting Out, Burning Out, Bowing Out: Stress and Survival on the Job*. Ontario, Canada: Financial Post Books, 1978.

Jackson, T. and Mayleas, D. *The Hidden Job Market: A System to Beat the System*. New York: Quadrangle Books, 1976.

Jameson, R.J. *The Professional Job-Changing System*. New Jersey: Performance Dynamics Publishing, 1978.

Kennedy, Marilyn Moats. *Career Knockouts: How to Battle Back*. Chicago: Follett Publishing, 1980.

Loughary, J.W. and Ripley, T.M. *Career and Life Planning Guide*. Chicago: Follett Publishing, 1976.

Machlowitz, Marilyn. *Workaholics: Living with Them, Working with Them*. Reading, MA: Addison–Wesley, 1980.

Molloy, John T. *Dress for Success*. Chicago: Follett Publishing, 1977.

Nash, K. *Get the Best of Yourself—How to Find Your Success Pattern and Make It Work for You*. New York: Grosset & Dunlap, 1976.

Parker, Allen and Ferrini, Paul. *Career Changes*. Technical Education Research Center, 44 Brattle St., Cambridge, MA 02138.

Uris, A. and Tarrant, J. *How to Keep from Getting Fired*. Chicago: Henry Regnery Company, 1975.

Yates, Jere E. *Managing Stress*. New York: AMACOM, 1980.

Working Smarter

Conklin, Robert. *How to Get People to Do Things*. Chicago: Contemporary Books, Inc., 1979.

Dale, Arbie M, *Twenty Minutes a Day to a More Powerful Intelligence*. New York: Playboy Press, n.d.

Dellinger, Susan and Deane, Barbara. *Communicating Effectively—A Complete Guide for Better Managing.* Radnor, PA: Chilton Book Co., 1980.

Douglas, Donna and Merrill, E. *Manage Your Time, Manage Your Work, Manage Yourself.* New York: AMACOM, 1980.

Flesch, Rudolf. *The Art of Readable Writing.* revised ed. New York: Harper and Row, 1979.

Flesch, Rudolf. *Say What You Mean.* New York: Harper and Row, 1972.

Frantz, Forrest H., Sr. *Successful Moonlighting Techniques That Can Make You Rich.* Englewood Cliffs, NJ: Parker Publishing Co., Inc., 1970.

Funk, Wilfred John, and Lewis, Norman. *Thirty Days to a More Powerful Vocabulary.* New York: Pocket, 1975.

Krump, Peter. *Breakthrough Rapid Reading.* Englewood Cliffs, NJ: Parker Publishing Co., Inc., 1979.

Lakein, Alan. *How to Get Control of Your Time and Your Life.* New York: Signet, 1974.

LeBoeuf, Michael. *Working Smart: How to Accomplish More in Half the Time.* New York: Warner Books, 1980.

LeBeouf, Michael. *Working Smartly.* New York: McGraw Hill, 1979.

Maberly, Norman C. *Mastering Speed Reading.* New York: Signet, 1973.

Mackenzie, R. Alex. *The Time Trap.* New York: McGraw Hill Book Co., 1975.

Moskowitz, Robert. *How to Organize Your Work and Your Life.* New York: Doubleday/Dolphin, 1981.

Nideffer, Robert M. and Sharpe, Roger. *Attention Control Training: How to Get Control of Your Mind Through Total Concentration.* New York: Wideview Books, 1979.

Power, Melvin. *Practical Guide to Better Concentration.* Hollywood, CA: Wilshire Book, n.d.

Swanick, John. *The Moonlighter's Manual.* Troy, NY: Moonlight Press, 1982.

Weisinger, Hendrie and Losenz, Norman M. *Nobody's Perfect: How to Give Criticism and Get Results.* New York: Stratford Press, 1982.

Winston, Stephanie. *Getting Organized.* New York: Warner Books, 1980.

Books and Organizations for Women on Working

Abarbanel, K., and Siegel, G.M. *Woman's Work Book.* New York: Praeger, 1975.

Angrist, S. and Almquist, E.M. *Careers and Contingencies.* Port Washington, NY: Kennirat Publ., 1975.

Baxter, Ralph H., Jr. *Sexual Harassment in the Workplace: A Guide to the Law.* Executive Enterprises Publ., Co., 33 W. 60th St., New York, NY.

Careers for Women, 43 West 61st St., New York, NY.

Careers for Women, Century Park Center, 9911 West Pico Blvd., Los Angeles, CA 90035. (213) 277-7754.

Careers for Women, 1 Hallidie Plaza, San Francisco, CA 94102. (415) 391-7613.

CHART, 123 East Grant St., Suite 1210, Minneapolis, MN 55403.

Dunlop, Jan. *Personal and Professional Success for Women.* Englewood Cliffs, NJ: Prentice-Hall, 1972.

Edulundi, S. and M. *Pick Your Job and Land It.* Santa Barbara, CA: Sandollar Press, 1973.

Flexible Career Associates, P.O. Box 6701, Santa Barbara, CA 93111.

Flexible Careers, 6 E. Monroe, #1502, Chicago, IL 60603.

Flexible Ways to Work, c/o YWCA, 1111 S.W. Tenth St., Portland, OR 97205.

Focus, 509 Tenth Avenue East, Seattle, WA.

Higginson, Margaret V., and Quick, Thomas L. *The Ambitious Woman's Guide to a Successful Career.* New York: AMACOM, 1975.

King, David, and Levine, Karen. *The Best Way in the World for a Woman to Make Money.* New York: Warner Books, 1980.

The League of Women Voters, 1730 M Street, NW, Washington, D.C. 20036.

Lemback, R. *A Checklist Guide to the Job Market: 1001 Job Ideas for Today's Woman.* Garden City, NY: Doubleday/Dolphin, 1975.

Molloy, John T. *The Women's Dress for Success Book.* Chicago: Follett, 1978.

New Ways to Work/Job Sharing Project, 149 Ninth Street, San Francisco, CA.

Ricci, Larry. *High-Paying Blue-Collar Jobs for Women*. New York: Ballantine, 1981.

Roesch, R. *There's Always a Right Job for Every Woman*. New York: Berkley Windhover Books, 1976.

Scholz, N.T.; Prince, J.S.; and Miller, G.P. *How to Decide: A Guide for Women*. New York: College Entrance Examination Board, 1975.

Wetherby, T. *Conversations—Working Women Talk about Doing a "Man's Job."* Millbrae, CA: Les Femmes Publishing, 1977.

Women Working at Home: The Homebased Business Guide and Directory. Scarsdale, NY: WWH Press.

Workshare, 311 East 50th St., New York, NY 10022.

Work Time Alternatives, P.O. Box 7514, Albuquerque, NM 87194.

Books to Help If You Are a Minority or Special-Interest-Group Member

U.S. Department of Interior, Bureau of Indian Affairs Publications: 1975. *Career Development Opportunities for Native Americans.*

Johnson, W.L. *Directory of Special Programs for Minority Group Members*. Garden Park, MD: Garrett Park Press, 1975.

Loughary, J.W. and Ripley, T.M. *Second Chance—Everybody's Guide to Career Change*. Eugene, OR: United Learning Corp., 1975.

Sprague, N. and Knatz, H.F. *Finding a Job: A Resource Book for the Middle-Aged and Retired*. Garden City, NY: Adelphi University Press, 1978.

Working Healthy

American Lung Association; American Cancer Society (New York Division), 19 West 56 St., New York, NY 10019.

Committee on Consumer Affairs, "Nonsmoker's Rights." New York County Lawyers' Association.

GASP Legal Fund (Group against Smokers' Pollution). *Non-smoking Employees' Guide to Preservation of Unemployment Insurance Benefits*, P.O. Box 1061, Berkeley, CA 94701.

Shimp, Donna. "Smoke-Free Work Area": Environmental Improvement Association, 111 Chestnut St., Salem, NJ 08079.

TECHNICAL
Peterson's *Engineering Science and Computer Jobs.* Princeton, NJ, 1982.

DATA PROCESSING
American Federation of Information Processing Societies, Inc., 1815 N. Lynn St., Arlington, VA 22209.

Byte and Creative Computing (monthly magazines for personal computer market).

Computerworld (weekly trade paper).

Datamation (monthly professional magazine).

"Office Machines and Computer Occupations," Occupational Outlook Handbook. U.S. Department of Labor.

"To Each His Own Computer," *Newsweek*, Feb. 27, 1982.

Zake, Rodney. "Your First Computer." In Computerland stores.

PERSONNEL
American Society for Personnel Administrators, 30 Park Drive, Berea, OH.

American Society for Training and Development, P.O. Box 5307, Madison, Wisc. 53705.

Personnel (bi-monthly professional magazine).

Personnel Administrator (monthly professional magazine).

Personnel Journal (monthly professional magazine).

Thinking about Work in General

Bormann, Ernest G., et al. *Interpersonal Communication in the Small Organization.* Englewood Cliffs, NJ: Prentice–Hall, 1969.

Carnegie, Dale. *How to Win Friends and Influence People.* New York: Pocket.

Crystal, John. *Where Do I Go from Here with My Life?* Berkeley, CA: Ten Speed Press, 1974.

Dyer, Wayne W. *Pulling Your Own Strings.* Funk and Wagnalls Publishing, 1978.

Kiev, Ari. *A Strategy for Success*. New York: Macmillan Publishing, 1977.

Laird, Donald A. and Laird, Eleanor. *Psychology: Human Relations and Motivation*. New York: McGraw–Hill, Gregg Division, 1972.

LeBoeuf, Michael. *Imagineering*. New York: McGraw–Hill, 1980.

Lynch, Edith M. *Decades: Lifestyle Changes in Career Expectations*. New York: AMACON, 1980.

May, Rollo. *The Courage to Create*. New York: W.W. Norton & Co., 1975.

Newman, Mildred, and Berkowitz, Bernie. *How to Be Your Own Best Friend*. New York: Random House, 1971.

Powell, Barbara. *Overcoming Shyness*. New York: McGraw–Hill, 1979.

Scheele, Adele M. *Skills for Success*. New York: Morrow, 1974.

Sheehy, Gail. *Passages*. New York: Bantam Books, 1977.

Shook, Robert L. *Winning Images*. New York: Macmillan Publishing, 1977.

Smith, Manuel J. *When I Say No, I Feel Guilty*. New York: Bantam, 1978.

Uris, Auren. *Executive Deskbook*. Van Nostrand Reinhold Co., 1970.

Weinberg, George. *Self-Creation*. New York: St. Martin's Press, 1978.

Useful Periodicals

Ad Search. National want-ad newspaper published each Saturday containing recruitment ads from help-wanted and business sections of nation's leading newspapers arranged according to job title. Write: Box 2083, Milwaukee, WI 53201.

Occupational Outlook Quarterly. United States Department of Labor, Bureau of Labor Statistics publication describing national outlook for various job types by quarter.

Index